PRAGUE

Roberta Bromley Etter
Photography by Tim Sharman

PASSPORT BOOKS
a division of *NTC Publishing Group*
Lincolnwood, Illinois USA

Published by Passport Books in conjunction with
The Guidebook Company Ltd.

This edition was first published in 1994 by Passport Books, a division of NTC Publishing Group,
4255 W. Touhy Avenue, Lincolnwood (Chicago), Illinois 60646-1975 U.S.A., originally published by
The Guidebook Company Ltd. © 1994 The Guidebook Company Ltd. All rights reserved.

ISBN: 0-8442-9672-4
Library of Congress Catalog Card Number: 93-71956

Editor: Sally-Anne Imémé
Series Editor: Anna Claridge
Illustrations Editor: Caroline Robertson
Design: De•Style Studio
Map Production: Periplus Cartographic Services, Singapore
Map Design: Tom Le Bas

Photography by Tim Sharman
Front cover by Tim Sharman; back cover by Lee Malis
Additional photography courtesy of Roberta Etter 4, 9, 18, 22, 31, 36, 37, 41, 44, 45, 47, 61, 102, 107, 139,
147, 159, 160, 162, 192; Karla Plicky from the author's collection 7, 66, 76, 82–83, 93, 99, 111, 124, 181;
Muzeum hlavního města Prahy 30, 38, 51; Christies South Kensington 143; Josef Lada 87, 88; Lee Malis
188–189

Production House: Twin Age Limited, Hong Kong
Printed in Hong Kong by Sing Cheong Printing Co Ltd

1520 Renaissance window and city arms, Old Town Hall

Author Roberta Bromley Etter is a freelance photojournalist and a regular contributor to *Executive Travel Magazine* on East European economy. She lived in Prague for several years, both before and after the Velvet Revolution, during which time she was correspondent for the *London Mail on Sunday* and *The Arkansas Gazette*. She also writes travel features and articles on antiques and folklore. Previous books include *Halley's Comet—Memories of 1910* and she is currently working on *Love Lore of the Pacific Rim*.

Fourteen years ago, writer and photographer Tim Sharman set out to discover the countries of eastern Europe, motivated by the general lack of information then available about the region. In 1980, he walked alone from the Baltic coast of Poland to Istanbul, an inspiring five-month trek which produced many long term friendships and enough photographs to launch what is now a large and busy picture library. His work has also been published in books, newspapers and magazines.

Jan Hus, martyred in 1415

Contents

Prague Castle and St Vitus' Cathedral from Malá strana, c. 1940

Introduction to Prague

The former Czechoslovakia was the marriage of convenience of two nations, the Czech and Slovak Federative Republics (CSFR), each with its own language and culture. From its formation in 1918 as a Slavic bloc between the Austrian and German empires, Czechoslovakia suffered the fate of grumbling spouses who agreed to disagree while waving the same flag. Now, after the official split of the two nations on 1 January 1993, Slovakia has her capital in Bratislava, only 45 kilometres (28 miles) from Vienna International Airport. The Czech Republic capital is Prague, one of the most majestic cities in the world.

Ask a person living in Prague how their city has changed and they would probably laugh—if they had time. Post-Velvet Revolution Prague is a completely different city. New places open almost daily. Old sites have taken on a glittery new veneer or even a new name. Former Communist-only hotels and spas are now open to the public. There are new places to gamble, new places to eat, new places to shop and even new places to learn about the old regime. Prague history has been rewritten. Former teachings of the old regime are no longer required and Prague's children are relearning new versions of their heritage. Prague is bursting to spread its wings and catch up with the Western world.

Despite the fact that many squares, metro stations and streets have had name changes, a tour guide is not necessary. All a person needs is a good pair of walking shoes and a bit of basic orientation. It is impossible not to feel the ghosts of Prague's colourful past as you prowl her fairy-tale streets. Just about every small winding street has some enchanting surprise, from random statues on rooftops to magical gardens hidden behind imposing walls.

The city itself is divided into five separate towns: **Staré město** (Old Town), **Nové Město** (New Town), **Malá Strana** (Lesser Town), **Hradčany** and **Josefov** (Jewish Town). To get to know Prague it must be carefully peeled like an onion and explored layer by layer according to the time available.

Architecture in Prague deserves special mention. Examples of virtually every period in history are preserved here and the paintings above many front doors describing the original function or owner of the house provide a fascinating sociological study.

Music lovers will enjoy wandering the streets where Mozart's eerie laughter is still said to be heard. The Jewish tradition is also strong in a city where Rabbi Löw created his Golem, forerunner of Frankenstein. The Jewish Museum is one of the most poignant in the world.

Whilst there are an endless amount of things to see and do during the day, nightlife is still limited. Casinos are thriving and there are a few floor shows and revues,

Dove headdress of a Bohemian Maiden, by H Whatley

but tourists should not expect Western style evening entertainment. Although a writer was elected president of the country, many of the Heroes of the Revolution are left facing a closed house. State subsidies no longer keep theatres out of the red and many have been shut down. However, *The Velvet Revolution*, a documentary, packs the house four times a day at the Albatross Theatre on Národní. It has become as popular with foreigners as the formerly taboo *Emmanuelle II* is with locals.

Street theatre, better known as people watching, is one of Prague's most rewarding pursuits. Society-seeking locals still prefer wine bars and coffee houses to the tourist-jammed discos, which were once considered the preserve of the young Communist élite and retain a certain undesirable stigma. There are century-old hang-outs where you can happily rub elbows with local artists, politicians, black marketeers, writers and friendly grandmothers. You will find that the locals love to talk and both beer (*pivo*) and wine (*víno*) are excellent topics to share.

After the Communist takeover in 1948, horse-drawn carriages were one of the many things considered far too bourgeois for the streets of Prague. Now the musical clip-clop of horses' hooves can be heard once again throughout the city. Some of the drivers wear top hats and tattered tails; some look as if they have just come from ploughing the fields. The variety of carts and carriages is endless. When winter arrives you can be sure of one thing: a large number of drivers will be wearing plain dark leather jackets, the well-known trademark of the former secret police.

Goethe once described Prague as the most beautiful jewel in the stone crown of the world. Though the jewel is in desperate need of polishing, it still ranks as one of Europe's most captivating cities—a city where every tourist can delight in searching out their own magic, mystery and intrigue.

The Velvet Revolution

There was nothing particularly extraordinary about the students gathered at Vyšehrad Cemetery on 27 October 1989 to mark the death of Jan Opletal, who died in 1938 demonstrating against Hitler's invasion. The police broke up this peaceful demonstration as they had done 50 years previously.

Times had changed since Opletal's death, most significantly in the 1980s with the arrival of Gorbachev in Moscow and the rise of Solidarity in Poland. For 20 years Czechoslovakia suffered at the hands of a regime they loathed, a regime that knew their distaste for violent resistance.

The government underestimated the students. With the East German Communist Party in collapse and leading dissident, Václav Havel, nominated for the Nobel Peace Prize, the thought of freedom was far stronger than fear. On 17 November 1989, the anniversary of Opletal's funeral, a student march in Prague developed into a nationwide anti-government protest.

At first the demonstrators were mostly young people. Theatre students joined in next and openly demanded an investigation into the police action. Within hours Prague theatres had voiced their support and in days all university faculties declared a strike. Taxi and tram drivers hooted their horns, shop workers wore tiny Czechoslovak flags, and even the Old Jewish Cemetery closed in protest. The students' demonstration was taken to the heart of this bitter nation and became the Velvet Revolution.

The first political party to form sprang from an alliance of dissident groups and called itself Civic Forum. In Slovakia another group emerged, Public Against Violence. The students threw themselves into the business of making a nation, demanding ever more resignations from the old regime, and more and more reforms. Declarations, speeches and appeals occurred daily. The young and the intelligentsia worked 24 hours a day: their fear of violence was almost palpable. Slowly the tide turned as increasing numbers of the working class joined the protest. By the end of the week, 700 enterprises and organizations had declared their support for Civic Forum.

The government began to crumble. The communists lost the force of their power. But the battle is still not over. Although Václav Havel has been re-elected president, many of the key positions are still filled by the old, unrevealing sea of chameleon faces.

The Czechs and Slovaks must now learn to live as free people in two separate nations, a people, as President Havel has said, who are 'Living within the Truth'.

Economic Developments

After 74 years of shaky marriage, no divorce could be really velvet. The Czechs and Slovaks are no exception. And though such notable figures as Britain's Prime Minister, John Major, have expressed the West's preference to deal with one Czechoslovakia rather than two infant republics, it was inevitable that the divorce would occur.

The Czechs have always acknowledged that their union with Slovakia came at a price. As the two republics veered in sharply different directions, however, that price became too high. While the Czechs have doggedly pressed ahead with free-market reforms, the Slovaks have drifted in indecision as unemployment rose to Western European levels and political leaders grasped at more autonomy. Given these strains, to imagine that this marriage could ever have been saved is little more than wishful thinking.

The Czechs, meanwhile, have faced their own problems. Mercedes Benz and Fiat SpA have postponed signing final agreements with truck manufacturers Avia-Liaz and Tatra as the Czech Government insisted on higher than market prices.

The fact is that without the Communists and under the firm leadership of Václav Klaus' right-wing Civic Democrats, the Czech Republic should be able to look forward to four years of political stability and economic growth. The Czech Republic has twice as many people, twice as much land, is responsible for three-quarters of the former federation's gross national product and industrial production. With just a fraction of Slovakia's unemployment, it has attracted US$540 million in foreign investment against the US$150 million placed in Slovakia.

Recently the EC agreed to extend some hope of eventual membership, and it has even been hinted that the Czech Republic could gain entry to the EC a lot quicker than the whole CSFR might have done. By the end of 1992, freed of the exigencies of the much poorer Slovakia, the Czech Republic was showing itself capable not just of economic survival, but also of achieving a degree of prosperity.

The financial crunch is already being felt and money is on the move. Vladimir Meciar, Slovakia's former Communist leader, dismissed in 1991 for using blackmail and secret police files, faces a much more difficult time in kick-starting the Slovak economy. Klaus, on the other hand, insisted on a federal policy based on strict monetarist principles. While there may be the same tariff policies and customs union, separate currencies, formed in February 1993, were inevitable.

Where the money goes, the people are not long in following. Ex-Slovak intelligentsia, including doctors, lawyers, professors and engineers, are already contributing to the increasing productivity of the Czech Republic. Foreign companies have opened offices in Prague as part of their huge investments, creating a healthy office market in which office space now rents at a square metre monthly rate comparable to New York.

The Prague Stock Exchange was founded on 9 July 1992 by 14 banks and five brokerage firms. Activity on the exchange began on 22 June 1993 with stocks traded on two major markets. One includes about 30 blue-chips and the other will eventually handle 300 second-tier companies. Between 40 and 50 brokerage firms have been authorized to trade.

The Czech Republic has also opened its first specialist mortgage bank in more than 40 years, the Czech Moravian Mortgage Bank. The new bank will offer mortgages on private housing, offices and small factories. The European Investment Bank has granted individual applicants over US$84 million to finance small and medium-sized projects.

Prague has so far undertaken the most ambitious mass privatisation programme of the post-Communist world. Privatising small businesses has proved relatively easy. An estimated 13,000 shops, cafés and the like had already been restored to their original owners or auctioned off to the highest bidder by early spring 1992. With big enterprises, preliminaries have been a bit more confusing.

Under the plan adopted, each of the former federation's 11 million adults had the right to sign up for a US$32 book of coupons, worth voucher points, that could be exchanged for shares in the companies of their choice. Some 8.6 million people elected to do so by the 29 February 1992 deadline, though nearly two-thirds of them have given their coupons to investment funds—the country's biggest growth industry—to invest on their behalf.

Companies for sale were listed, with remarkably scanty details, to help the population make their selection and bid voucher points. The choices were made by luck of the draw rather than actual knowledge. Now that shares are distributed through a series of computerized auctions, the new owners are free to sell them to anyone. A second and last wave of voucher-driven privatization is planned by the end of 1993. With the separation of the Czech and Slovak Republics, plans have been altered to include both Czech and Slovak companies in the voucher scheme. Many teething problems have been encountered, to the great dismay of Václav Klaus, who is fond of repeating, 'When you drive through the mud, you do not slow down'.

While the European Bank of Reconstruction and Development has doled out US$157 million to Eastern Europe, the real Western money has come from businesses and investors who have ploughed US$7 billion into the Czech Republic, Poland and Hungary over the past three years.

Essential infrastructure projects such as better roads and telephone systems, necessary to bring the country up to the level of Western Europe are already in hand. Although the Americans have reached a position of far greater decisive influence in

TIPS FOR DOING BUSINESS IN THE CZECH REPUBLIC

DO   either plan to spend an inordinate amount of time in Prague or find a local agent to keep a hands-on interest in transactions.

DO   read the local English language newspapers to keep abreast of current business events. The *Prague Post* is the best on offer.

DON'T rush business transactions. The Czechs still have much to learn and undue pressure can spoil a deal.

DON'T assume that such concepts as marketing, free-market and advertising are instantly understood.

the conversion of the Czech economy, there is also strong investment from many European nations. Kleinwort Benson, a London-based consulting firm, has been selected to help the Czech government choose a company to construct and operate an 83-kilometre (51-mile) toll highway between Plzeň and Rozvadov, the Czech–German border crossing. Twenty-three foreign road builders were selected to bid on a project that will not only gain the rights to collect tolls, but also to manage the service stations and other businesses along the route.

Johnson Partnership, architects, planners, engineers and quantity surveyors, mounted an exhibition of work in Prague in May 1990. Two years later, it had notched up an impressive amount of work in the CSFR and established a joint-venture partnership with Hexaplan, a newly privatized firm of architects and engineers in Brno. Their most notable contract to date is the refurbishment of the Australian embassy, chancery and ambassador's residence in Prague.

Another London firm, Rothschilds & Sons, has served as federal advisor on the privatization of the gas pipeline running through the former Czechoslovakia from the CIS. This project, a source of heated argument between the Czechs and Slovaks, determined which authority had the right to sell off the Transgas company.

Though construction has suffered a 33 per cent drop in the past two years, the urgent need for new hotels is seen as offering a possible halt to the decline. The Ministry of Foreign Trade has selected 12 landmark buildings to be transformed into first-class hotels. New projects are currently underway by the Taj group, Ritz-Carlton, Holiday Inn and others. Some 200 foreign companies competed to operate the former Communist élite Hotel Praha, which has been refurbished as part of a scheme that includes up to 30,000 square metres of new office space.

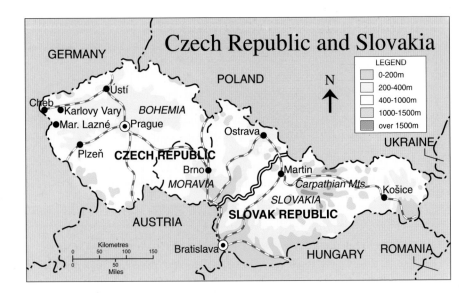

In an ironic twist, the Czech Republic is finding that its bilateral Europe Agreement with the EC can be more of a hindrance than a help. On the one hand the EC is helping to improve productivity, while on the other it is protecting its own by throwing up extra-high tariff barriers to raise the price of competitive goods. Despite the fact the Republic is working at reducing subsidies to its industries, now said to be on a scale comparable with EC levels, yet higher sales tariffs on products like steel, chemicals, textiles, glass and agriculture serve to limit access to neighbouring markets. As a result, where once the EC ran a trade deficit with Eastern Europe, in 1992 it piled up a US$3 billion surplus.

Though Czechs have been flirting with the idea of forming their own common market with Poland and Hungary, this plan, inspired by the need to protect their fledgling economies, is moving in fits and starts.

Observers predict a mixed outlook for the country; while expected to post modest gains, Czechs have had to deal with price rises after the introduction of a 23 per cent value-added tax on most items in the New Year, and dig deeper for new health and welfare taxes. Unemployment, which was 2.9 per cent in 1992, is expected to double by the end of this year as some newly privatized companies go bust.

The infant government of the Czech Republic claims it can modernize its economy to EC standards by 1995. Those hoping to do business in Prague, however, would do well to remember the few pointers listed as dos and don'ts.

Facts for the Traveller

Getting There

BY AIR

Ruzyně Airport is located 20 kilometres (12 miles) outside Prague. There are only two luggage belts so the wait can be appreciable. Porters and trolleys are available and customs and immigration procedures have become fairly painless.

ČSA Československé Aerolinie (ČSA), the national carrier, now offers direct flights to most major cities of the world. Air France bought 40 per cent of the airline in 1992 and flight slots to some cities have almost doubled as a consequence.

Taxi prices from the airport into the city can vary drastically. Officially the rate should be around 100 crowns (kčs). It is usually closer to 300 or 400 kčs. Prices should be agreed before leaving the airport. ČSA provides a bus transfer service from the airport to their main terminal at náměstí Republiky, cost 4 kčs plus 1 kčs for each piece of luggage. There is a ČSA information desk at the airport. If you are not a stranger to Prague you can take local bus No 119 (4 kčs) which ends at the metro station Dejvická (by the Diplomat Hotel).

BY CAR

If you are travelling by car a current driving licence and proof of insurance coverage are obligatory. Though petrol coupons are no longer required, it is good to remember that most stations do not take credit cards and only accept Czech currency. Petrol prices correspond to European pricing. There is limited availability for service and repairs and spares for Western-made cars are difficult to find and expensive. If you are driving at night, it is advisable to have sufficient petrol as stations are often difficult to find (see Useful Addresses, page 176).

A few points to remember:
- Speed limits are strictly enforced in the Czech Republic. In towns, the speed limit is 60 kilometres (37 miles), outside towns it is 110 kilometres (56 miles) per hour. Fines are payable on the spot and can be somewhat unreasonable.
- There is no toll on motorways, but seat belts are obligatory when motorway driving.
- There is an absolute ban on drunk driving in the Czech Republic. You risk losing your driving licence or facing a criminal conviction. Recently, severe fines have consistently been levied.
- Passport inspection at the border posts still tends to be quite lengthy and thorough.

By Rail

There are three international railway stations in Prague: train travellers can arrive at Praha-Holešovice in the north of the city or Praha-Hlavní nádraží and Praha-Masarykovo nádraží, both of which are close to the city centre.

Tickets can be purchased for both national and international travel, first or second class, although accommodation tends to be quite a bit below European standards. You must pay for tickets in Czech crowns if purchased at the station or in any Western currency at Čedok offices.

Taxis are generally available at railway stations, though porters and trolleys are not. All three stations connect with the metro—at Praha-Hlavní nádraží the entrance is in the main ticket hall.

There are left-luggage offices at each of the three main railway stations. The weight limit per piece is 15 kilograms (33 pounds) and the charge is currently 1 kč per piece per day. Lockers are also available.

Many of Prague's new homeless have taken up residency in Hlavní nádraží. Be careful of your belongings and never leave bags unattended.

Train arrival and departure information is posted at every railway station. A foreigner might have difficulty deciphering the timetables, as all symbols are explained in Czech, so use the information office at Hlavní nádraží, second floor, right hand corner (on metro line C). There is often a queue but it is usually worth the wait. Fairly reliable information will be given in English about any train connections.

A minimum of five trains a day connect Prague with every larger town in the country. Train categories are: Slow—dirt cheap but stops at every station. Tickets for these trains can be purchased either at the station or from the conductor on the train; Fast—basic fare plus 16 kčs; International—for these you need a seat reservation (Hlavní nádraží, reservations office, first floor). There are no refreshments sold on slow trains. Buffet or restaurant cars are usually attached to most long-distance trains.

Public conveniences on the trains are often poorly equipped. Be sure to take your own toilet paper with you on the journey.

Long-distance trains are often delayed by as much as one hour or more in winter.

When To Go

Prague is a city blessed with four distinct seasons. Summer months are generally sunny and warm. Winters are cold with rain and snow. Spring and autumn are mild but changeable.

Looking east from the Old Town Hall tower to the Powder Tower

Costumes; St John's Day in Prague by Walter Crane (above); south Bohemian dress by M Ales (below)

	Average Daily Temperature				Average Daily Rainfall	
	Min		Max			
	°C	°F	°C	°F	mm	inches
Jan	-5	23	0	31	18	0.7
Feb	-4	24	1	34	18	0.7
Mar	-1	30	7	44	18	0.7
Apr	4	38	12	54	27	1.1
May	8	46	18	64	48	1.9
Jun	11	52	21	70	64	2.5
Jul	13	55	23	73	68	2.7
Aug	13	55	22	72	59	2.2
Sep	9	49	18	64	37	1.4
Oct	5	41	11	53	39	1.5
Nov	1	33	6	42	20	0.8
Dec	-3	27	1	34	21	0.8

Visas and Passports

Every visitor to the Czech Republic must have a passport that is valid for at least five months. Visas are no longer required for visitors holding EC or American passports. You are also no longer required to register your presence with the police and it is possible to stay in private residences.

Customs Regulations

There is no duty on the import of your personal items, which include: 2 litres of wine, 1 litre of spirits, 250 cigarettes (or the equivalent in cigars or tobacco), 1,000 shotgun pellets or 50 rifle bullets.

The above quantities and items may be exported duty free. You can also export gifts with a value up to 1,000 kčs, and any goods purchased with foreign currency in a Tuzex shop. Be sure to keep all receipts for your purchases. There is some fluctuation in the export laws, so be sure to enquire when you make a purchase. In 1991, a little known law was enacted requiring 300 per cent duty on crystal chandeliers: quite a hefty surprise when you cross the border.

For up-to-date information contact your nearest Čedok office, customs offices on border crossings or the Central Customs Authority in Prague, tel 232 22 70.

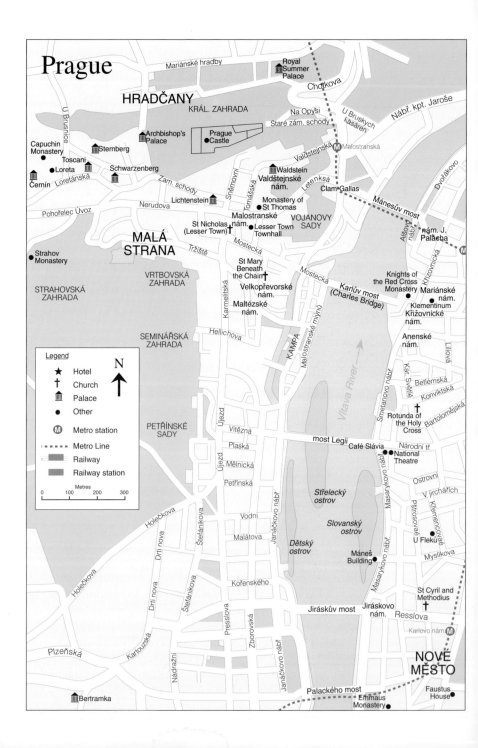

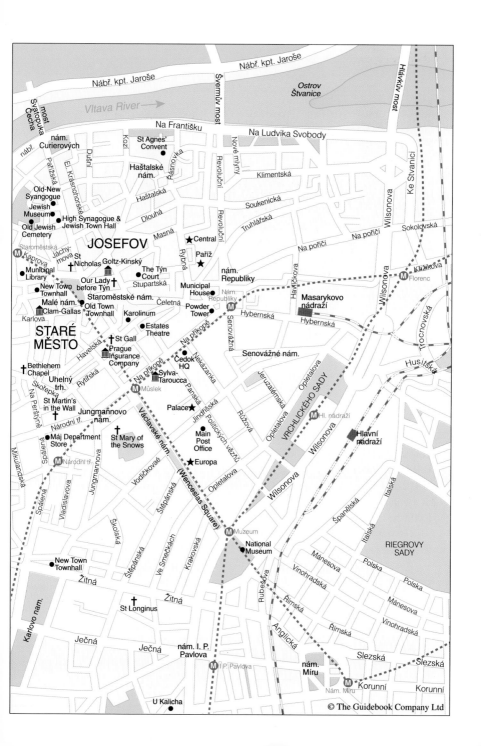

Nábř. kpt. Jaroše

Nábř. kpt. Jaroše

Ostrov
Štvanice

Hlávkův most

most
Svatopluka
Čecha

nábř.

Vltava River →

Na Františku

Na Ludvika Svobody

nám.
Curierových

Pařížská

E. Krásnohorské

Dušní

Kozí

St Agnes'
Convent

Haštalské
nám.

Nové mlýny

Revoluční

Klimentská

Rásnovka

Soukenická

Ke Stvanici

Wilsonova

Sokolovská

Old-New
Syangogue

Haštalská

Jewish
Museum

Dlouhá

Jáchy-
mova

High Synagogue &
Jewish Town Hall

Truhlářská

Na poříčí

Na poříčí

Old Jewish
Cemetery

Masná

Revoluční

Křižíkova

Staroměstská

Florenc

Kaprova

★Central

Rybná

JOSEFOV

St
Nicholas Goltz-Kinský

Paříž
★

nám.
Republiky

Havlíčkova

Wilsonova

Municipal
Library

The Týn
Court

Stupartská

Masarykovo
nádraží

New Town
Townhall

Our Lady
before Týn

Municipal
House

Nám.
Republiky

Malé nám.

Staroměstské nám.

Čeletná

Hybernská

Hybernská

Clam-Gallas

Old Town
Townhall

Karolinum

Powder
Tower

Senovážná

Karlova

STARÉ
MĚSTO

Estates
Theatre

Na příkopě

Husitská

Trocnovská

St Gall

Senovážné nám.

Havelská

Prague
Insurance
Company

Na příkopě

Cedok
HQ

Nekázanka

Jeruzalémská

Opletalova

VRCHLICKÉHO SADY

Wilsonova

Bethlehem
Chapel

Rytířská

Sylva-
Taroucca

Panská

Uhelný
trh.

Skořepka

Můstek

Palace★

Jindřišská

Politických věznů

Růžová

Hl. nádraží

St Martin's
in the Wall

Jungmannovo
nám.

Na Perštýně

Main
Post
Office

Hlavní
nádraží

Národní tř.

Máj Department
Store

St Mary of
the Snows

Europa★

Opletalova

Italská

Spálená

Národní tř.

Vodičkovaé

Wilsonova

Vladislavova

Jungmannova

Štěpánská

(Wenceslas Square)

Opletalova

Španělská

Italská

Muzeum

Mikulandská

Školská

Václavské nám.

National
Museum

RIEGROVY
SADY

New Town
Townhall

Štěpánská

Ve Smečkách

Krakovská

Mánesova

Polska

Polska

Žitná

Rubešova

Vinohradská

Mánesova

Karlovo nám.

Žitná

Vinohradská

St Longinus

Ječná

Ječná

nám. I. P.
Pavlova

Anglická

Římská

Římská

Slezská

Slezská

I.P. Pavlova

nám.
Míru

Korunní

Korunní

Nám. Míru

U Kalicha

© The Guidebook Company Ltd

Na příkopě, built in 1760, from Wenceslas Square with the Powder Tower

Money

The basic monetary unit in the Czech Republic is the Czech crown (kčs), which is divided into units of five, ten, 20 and 50 hellers. Crown coins come in denominations of 1, 2 and 5, which you will need to purchase tickets for local transport and for use in telephones. Banknotes come in denominations of 10, 20, 50, 100, 500, 1,000 and 5,000. Be careful of the 20 and 1,000 kč notes as they are a very similar blue colour. Also be warned of old money. The 100 kč note depicting former President Gottwald is no longer valid.

Payment by cheque is unheard of in the Czech Republic. Most hotels now take credit cards but often a restaurant will not. Traveller's cheques may be changed at banks and currency exchange offices. You will need to show your passport when exchanging traveller's cheques. There is no longer a minimum exchange requirement to enter the country.

Black market money changers crowd the area around Wenceslas Square (Václavské náměstí). However, the official exchange rate is so close to the black market rate that it is not worth the risk. The black market is a good place to be short changed or given out-of-circulation banknotes. It is also illegal to change money in this way, though the police are not as rigid as they once were.

Chequepoint currency exchange offices are found at several locations. One of the largest is on Old Town Square (Staroměstské náměstí). Be sure to check the commission rate to make sure it seems reasonable. Your hotel will also usually exchange smaller amounts of cash, though banks offer better rates. (For banks and exchange offices see Useful Addresses page 167.)

Communications

TELEPHONE

After more than 40 years of centrally planned neglect, the Czech Republic is realizing that without decent communications their economy may never recover. 'In Prague half the country is waiting for a telephone,' one joke runs, 'the other half is waiting for a dial tone.'

More to the point, after searching the town for a telephone booth, the likelihood of its working is very slim. For a foreigner, the best place to make a telephone call without incurring added hotel charges is a post office. There you will find coin boxes or a *telefon* office with an operator. Write the number you wish to call on a piece of paper and hand it to the operator. When the operator has connected the call they will direct you to a booth where you pick up the receiver and talk to your party. You pay the charges at the end of the call. International calls are fairly expensive: a three-minute call to London, for example, will cost 95 kčs. You will be charged for a minimum of three minutes even if the call is shorter. Should you make an international call from a private home it is considered very proper to offer to pay.

Local calls in Prague cost a flat rate of 1 kč, no matter how long your conversation. For local calls placed through the operator, dial 102 or 108.

FAX

The same office that handles telephone calls at the post office will be able to send a fax. The sign will read *telefax* and a similar procedure must be followed. Sending a fax is not instantaneous, however. You must leave the papers with the operator and return at a later time when you will be informed of the charges.

TELEGRAMS

In a country with few telephones, sending local telegrams is common practice and very cheap. Telegrams are either sent at a post office, where you pay directly, or from a private telephone, where they are billed. Telegrams will be delivered to the addressee within one or two hours, the following morning at the latest. Overseas telegrams conform with overseas telephone charges.

LETTERS AND POSTCARDS

Letters and postcards can be mailed at the post office or in the yellow postboxes located on many street corners. Collection times are written on each postbox. Inland rates are: 3 kčs for letters, 1 kč for postcards. European rates: for postcards 3 kčs, letters 4 kčs. Overseas rates: 5 kčs postcards and 6 kčs letters. Stamps can be purchased at post offices, hotels and tobacconists.

Parcels can be mailed at the post office parcel counter. Small gift parcels (books, records, slides, etc) are duty free. Postal rates are on display at every post office but you will find that the cost of sending a gift is often less than the charge for shipping. The railway station Praha-Masarykovo on Hybernská has a 24-hour parcel service.

The main post office (Hlavní pošta) at Jindrisská 14, near Wenceslas Square (Václavské náměstí) open 24 hours a day. Other post offices are open from 08:00–18:00, Monday to Friday, and 08:00–12:00 on Saturday.

Transportation

All public transport is state owned and heavily subsidized. The nationwide network of trains, buses and all local town transport (tram, bus and metro in Prague) is well developed and inexpensive.

BUS

The network of bus lines is very dense and usually runs according to schedule. Fares are cheap and normally collected by the driver for inter-city runs. Short-distance buses tend to be crowded during rush hours (06:00–08:00 and 14:00–17:00). Tickets for long distance buses (with seat reservation) are booked at the bus terminal (Florenc metro station, Sokolovská, line C). The bus driver will sell you a ticket for any non-reserved seats ten minutes before departure. Long-distance buses have a refreshment break of about 20 minutes en route. Buses are comfortable, safe and clean.

Prague city buses need a bit more study to learn the routes. You can pick up a schedule at the bus terminal.

METRO

You travel fastest and safest in Prague with the metro. It runs along three lines, A, B and C, which are different colours. Maps of the metro are on display in every com-

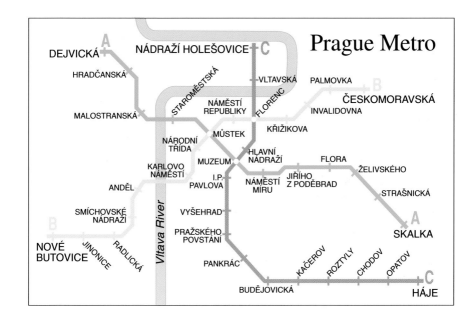

partment of the train. Individual stations will give you an idea of the location of the various sites and all entrances to the metro stations are clearly marked. You use the same 4 kč tickets (bought from a slot machine or Tabac) that you use for the tram or bus. All tickets must be punched: punch machines are in every bus, tram and the hall of every metro station. You must hold onto your ticket until the end of the journey and there is an immediate 500 kč fine for not having a punched ticket. Slot machines take 1, 2, and 5 kč coins. There is a tourist ticket that gives unlimited travel for six days for 35 kčs and seven days, 40 kčs. The ticket is obtainable from PNS shops, one of which is located in the hall of the metro station Hradčanská on line A. The metro runs from 05:00–24:00. If you miss the last metro you can use either a night tram or a night bus which run approximately every 30–40 minutes.

TAXIS

Taxi drivers in Prague are notorious. If you speak Czech they are usually cheap and efficient. If you do not, be prepared to pay some high prices. Travelling within the city you should never pay more than 40 kčs, to the outskirts or back about 80 kčs. Taxis may be ordered by telephone, for 20 to 30 kčs more. There should be no extra charge for baggage. Try only to take a taxi with a working meter and pay what the fare reads. Tipping is approximately ten per cent.

TRAMS

Tram lines run by most of the major tourist attractions and are a good way to see the city for only 4 kčs. Tram No 22 goes by Máj Department store all the way to Prague Castle.

Holidays

New Year's Day	1 January
Easter Monday	March/April
May Day	1 May
Liberation Day	8 May
National Day	5 July
National Day	28 October
Reconciliation Day	1 November
Christmas	24–25 December
St Stephen's Day	26 December

Shopping

Prague shops are open at different times. Department stores are open from 08:00–19:00, food shops from 07:00–20:00. Private shops open from 09:00–18:00 (with exceptions), and state shops from 08:00–12:00, 14:00–18:00. Most shops are closed at the weekends with the exception of some privately owned shops. For specific shops, see Useful Addresses page 176.

Sports

BICYCLE RENTAL
Cyklocentrum
Karlovo náměstí 29, Prague 2. Open 09:00–18:00, Monday to Friday and Saturday from 08:00–13:00. Mountain bikes rent for 250 kčs a day.

Old Town Square Bike Rental is an outdoor stand in front of the Church of St Nicholas (Kostel sv Mikuláše). Touring bikes are 130 kčs a day.

Take Tram No 9 to Vozovna Motel and walk several minutes to Nad Zameckem 379/ 60 to a small stand renting bikes in front of a pedicab stand. Touring bikes rent for 100 kčs per day. They will direct you to Cibulka Park, where there are several bike trails.

■ BIKING HOLIDAYS
Geotour is a company specializing in tailor-made holidays, including cross-country biking. Contact director Zdeňek Kukal at Storkanová 11, Prague 5. Tel/Fax (02) 53 34 55.

GOLF

Golf can be played in Prague, only minutes from the centre of the city, on an extensive golf course above the Golf Hotel in Prague's western borough of Motol. The exit road at Stodulky from the Prague–Plzeň motorway leads to the club house. The course is open from 1 April to 30 October, from 08:00–20:00. Out of season, if playing conditions are good, from 09:00 to nightfall. Green fees, payable to the greenkeeper, are for one day, one week or a longer period. For membership, apply to Golf Club Prague, Na Morání 4, Prague 2.

HORSE RACING

State Racecourse Prague 5, Velká Chuchle. Tel 231 25 94/231 03 96. The racing season starts in April, with races every Sunday.

WALKING

The countryside around Prague is peppered with trails, some even passing within the city boundaries, and rambling is a favoured weekend pastime for city dwellers. There is no English language walking guide, but you should obtain the relevant map covering your intended walk showing the colour-coded trails.

English Language Books

While there are numerous bookshops in Prague, they actually serve more as a quiet refuge from the summer hordes of tourists than as havens of mind-expansion if your Czech is not up to par. There are very few shops that do sell English-language books, with the exception of a few guides, and the prices at those that do may overstep your budget for an entire day.

For an admirable selection of English classics, plays, mysteries, guides and recent

paperback best sellers, go to Zahran-
icni Literatura, located at Vodičkova
41 (the street where the trams cut
through Wenceslas Square (Václavské
náměstí), Prague 1. Prices start
around 150 kčs. Right around the corner, inside the Alfa complex at
Václavské náměstí 28, you will find a
smaller version of the above with
about half the selection. Artia has a
bookshop at Ve Smečkách 30 with a
wide selection of foreign maps and
travel books.

English Language Films

Marquees are scarce and neon thank-
fully non-existent, but Prague does
have a dozen or more cinemas tucked
away between the spires and castles of
the downtown area.

Check the weekly guide in your
hotel for the current film or drop by
the theatre and look on the board
posted at the front for the week's
offerings (see Useful Addresses on
page 170).

Libraries

The **American Library** of the United
States Embassy houses a collection of
books, magazines and newspapers
ranging from politics to music, architecture to sports. Everyone is welcome

Basilica of St George (above); detail from the Palace of the Archbishop of Prague (below)

to enter, browse and read, but due to a shortage of funds, only Czech citizens may borrow books. Library cards can be obtained at the front desk.

In addition to reading material, the library owns a collection of videos that are shown free throughout the month. For the current film schedule, stop by Vlašská 11 in Prague 1, just up the street from the embassy, or call 53 66 41 for information.

The library is open Monday to Thursday from 10:00–17:00 and Friday from 10:00–15:00.

The **Klementinum** complex (Klementinum 190, Mariánské náměstí) houses the National and Technical libraries and a good collection of British and American literature.

The English section is sponsored by the British Council and has more than 22,000 volumes of British reference material, fiction, non-fiction and periodicals. Every Wednesday at 15:30 they show British films.

The hours are Monday, Wednesday and Friday 09:00–15:00, Tuesday and Thursday 13:00–19:00. Tel 26 65 41 for more information.

Calendar dial of the Astronomical Clock (above); Old Town Hall door detail (below)

The Towns of Prague

For a thousand years, kings and queens passed through the land known as Bohemia. Some made it their home, some only their possession. All have left their mark in one form or another.

The capital of Bohemia, Prague, is the unique combination of natural beauty and unsurpassed architecture spanning those ten centuries. Though now officially divided into ten separate districts, it is the five historic towns dating from the days of Charles IV (1346–1378) that give Prague its character.

Malá strana bridge tower and Hradčany from Charles Bridge

At the beginning of the 19th century Prague was a city of 80,000 souls. The area experienced steady growth until just before World War I when the population reached over half a million. After the war the city mushroomed: its area tripled in size and the numerous districts were born. These days, spread on either side of the Vltava, Prague has grown to 1,200,000 inhabitants occupying an area of 215 square miles (550 square kilometres).

The most densely developed portion, on the heights overlooking the rest of the city, is the ancient district of **Hradčany**, home of Prague Castle (Pražský hrad), the Loreta and Strahov Monastery (Strahovský klášter). Below it lie **Malá strana** (Lesser Town) and the island of Kampa, which were crowded with ostentatious palaces during the 13th century.

On the other side of the river is **Staré město** (Old Town), one of Europe's best preserved medieval capitals. The narrow lanes echo with history, most poignantly in **Josefov** or the Jewish Quarter. Next to Staré město is **Nové město**, or New Town, an area rich in parks and gardens. Here the designs of Charles IV and his architects are most obvious. The wide open spaces and sweeping boulevards such as Wenceslas Square (Václavské náměstí) are known the world over.

Unification of the city was not accomplished until the rule of Emperor Josef II (1765–1790). Before that time each of the districts had its own architecturally superb town hall. Even today the districts have distinct flavours, which complement as well as contrast each other to form the political, economic and cultural capital of the country.

A sweeper in Staré město, 1930

Chronology of Events

5th century AD   Advent of the Slavníkovci tribes to the territory of Prague.

9th century AD   Battle for supremacy between the Slavníkovci and the Přemysl.

870   Founding of Prague Castle by the Přemysl.

890s   Founding of the first church at Prague Castle.
Prague Castle becomes the seat of the Czech princes.

965   First written description, by merchant Ibrahim Ibn-Jacob, of the town of Prague as a lively market place.

972   Bohemia becomes part of the Holy Roman Empire.

973   Founding of the Prague bishopric under Boleslav.

1055–1061   Expulsion of German merchants.
Construction of St Vitus' Basilica.

1070   Founding of Vyšehrad.

1120–1142   Construction boom and spread of Romanesque style.

1170   Building of first stone bridge (Judith Bridge).

1230   Staré město receives its town charter.
King Wenceslas I begins fortification of Staré město.

1257   Founding of Malá strana.

14th century   The rule of the Přemysl in Bohemia ends.

1338   King John of Luxembourg grants permission for the construction of the Old Town Hall.

1344   Prague is promoted to an archbishopric.
Construction begins on St Vitus' Cathedral at Prague Castle.

(preceding pages) Charles Bridge from Staré město bridge tower. Petřín Hill is on the left with the twin spires of Strahov Monastery breaking the centre left skyline

1348	Charles IV founds the first university in central Europe and Nové město. Building begins on Petřín Hill.
1357	Commencement of the building of Charles Bridge (Karlův most).
1391	Bethlehem Chapel (Betlémská kaple) is founded.
1398	Jan Hus is appointed as Magister Primarius.
1402	Jan Hus preaches his first service at Bethlehem Chapel against the secularization of the church.
1415	Jan Hus is burned at the stake.
1419	Death of Wenceslas IV. Hussite storming of Carthusian monastery.
1486–1502	Building of Vladislav Hall at Prague Castle.
1538–1563	Building of Royal Summer Palace.
1526	Hapsburg Archduke Ferdinand I is crowned King of Bohemia.
1541	The Great Fire of Prague.
1546	Ferdinand I goes to war against the German princes.
1583	Prague becomes the official residence of the Hapsburgs.
1584–1612	Prague becomes the seat of the imperial court of Rudolf II and world centre for art and artists.
1618	Defenestration of Prague governors. Beginning of the insurrection of the Bohemian Estates. Beginning of Thirty Years' War.
1620	Defeat of the insurrection of the Bohemian Estates at the Battle of White Mountain.

1624–1630	Building of Wallenstein Palace (Valdštejn palác).
1648	Last military action of the Thirty Years' War, the siege of the town by the Swedes.
1653–1728	Building of the Klementinum.
1704–1755	Beginning of baroque style in Prague. Construction of the Church of St Nicholas (Kapela sv Mikuláše).
1740–1780	Rule of Maria Theresa.
1740–1790	Return of religious freedom to Bohemia.
1780–1790	Rule of Joseph II.
1781	Construction of Týl Theatre (now Estates Theatre).
1784	Unification of the four towns of Prague.
1787	Première of Mozart's *Don Giovanni* .
1788	Founding of first general hospital.
1791	First industrial exhibition.

Ruins of Prague Bridge during the flood of 1890

1818	Founding of the National Museum.
1838–1848	Reconstruction of the Old Town Hall.
1868	Founding of the National Theatre.
1876	Founding of the Rudolfinum.
1881	Opening of the National Theatre and, three months later, the fire which destroyed it.
1883	Reopening of the National Theatre.

Vladimir Ilyich Lenin in 1919, the year he formed the Comintern

1890   First May Day demonstration in Prague.

1893   Opening of the Bohemian National Museum.

1912   Prague conference of the Russian Socialist Democratic Party chaired by Lenin.

28 Oct 1918   Czechoslovakia becomes an independent state.

14 Nov 1918   Tomaš Masaryk becomes first president of the Republic.

1933   Sudetendeutsche Heimatfront (Sudeten German Home Party) is founded by Konrad Henlein.
Building of Strahov Stadium.

30 Sept 1938   Chamberlain, Daladier, Mussolini and Hitler sign the Munich Agreement sacrificing Czechoslovakia.

Celebration of the 1,000th anniversary of the death of St Wenceslas, Wenceslas Square.
President Tomás Masaryk is in the middle of the procession

22 Oct 1938	President Beneš goes into exile in England.
1939	Occupation of Prague by Nazi Germans. Establishment of the Protectorate of Bohemia and Moravia.
1945	Soviet Red Army liberates Prague. American troops are prohibited from entering by the Treaty of Yalta.
1948	Communist take over.
1953	First television broadcast in Prague. Death of Josef Stalin.
1960	Prague becomes the capital of the Czechoslovak Socialist Republic.
1963	Near collapse of whole economy.

1966	First work on metro system begins.
1968	'Socialism with a human face' is developed under the leadership of Alexander Dubček. Prague Spring movement. Occupation of Czechoslovakia by troops of the Warsaw Pact.
1968–1969	Soviet occupation of Czechoslovakia. Stagnation of economy.
1975	Playwright Václav Havel writes an open letter to Gustav Husák pointing out the decline of the country.
1976	Charter 77 is founded to oppose abuse of human rights.
1980s	Rise of Solidarity in Poland. Arrival of Gorbachev in Moscow.
17 Nov 1989	The Velvet Revolution—rebirth of democracy.
Oct 1992	The Velvet divorce proceedings begin.
1 Jan 1993	Official separation of Czechoslovakia into the Czech Republic and Slovakia.

The Power of Fear

The basic question one must ask is this: why are people in fact behaving in the way they do? Why do they do all these things that, taken together, form the impressive image of a totally united society giving total support to its government? For any unprejudiced observer, the answer is, I think, self-evident: they are driven to it by fear.

For fear of losing his job, the schoolteacher teaches things he does not believe; fearing for his future, the pupil repeats them after him; for fear of not being allowed to continue his studies, the young man joins the Youth League and participates in whatever of its activities are necessary; fear that, under the monstrous system of political credits, his son or daughter will not acquire the necessary total of points for enrolment at a school leads the father to take on all manner of responsibilities and 'voluntarily' to do everything required. Fear of the consequences of refusal leads people to take part in elections, to vote for the proposed candidates and to pretend that they regard such ceremonies as genuine elections; out of fear for their livelihood, positions or prospects, they go to meetings, vote for every resolution they have to, or at least keep silent: it is fear that carries them through sundry humiliating acts of self-criticism and penitence and the dishonest filling out of a mass of degrading questionnaires; fear that someone might inform against them prevents them from giving public, and often even private, expression to their true opinions. It is the fear of suffering financial reverses and the effort to better themselves and ingratiate themselves with the authorities that in most cases makes working men put their names to 'work commitments'; indeed, the same motives often lie behind the establishment of Socialist Labour Brigades, in the clear realization that their chief function is to be mentioned in the appropriate reports to higher levels. Fear causes people to attend all those official celebrations, demonstrations and marches. Fear of being prevented from continuing their work leads many scientists and artists to give allegiance to ideas they do not in fact accept, to write things they do not agree with or know to be false, to join official organizations or to take part in work of whose value they have the lowest opinion, or to distort and mutilate their own works.

In the effort to save themselves, many even report others for doing to them what they themselves have been doing to the people they report...

...The question arises, of course, what are people actually afraid of? Trials? Torture? Loss of property? Deportations? Executions? Certainly not. The most brutal forms of pressure exerted by the authorities upon the public are, fortunately, past history—at least in our circumstances. Today, oppression takes more subtle and choice forms. And even if political trials do not take place today—everyone knows how the authorities manage to manipulate them—they only represent an extreme threat, while the main thrust has moved into the sphere of existential pressure. Which, of course, leaves the core of the matter largely unchanged.

Notoriously, it is not the absolute value of a threat which counts, so much as its relative value. It is not so much what a man objectively loses, as the subjective importance it has for him on the plane on which he lives,

Václav Havel, President of the Czech Republic

with its own scale of values. Thus, if a man today is afraid, say, of losing the chance of working in his own field, this may be a fear equally as strong, and productive of the same reactions, as if—in another historical context— he had been threatened with the confiscation of his property. Indeed, the technique of existential pressure is, in a sense, more universal. For there is no one in our country who is not, in a broad sense, existentially vulnerable. Everyone has something to lose and so everyone has reason to be afraid. The range of things a man can lose is a very wide one, extending from the manifold privileges of the ruling caste and all the special opportunities afforded to the powerful—such as the enjoyment of undisturbed work, advancement and earning power, the ability to work at all in one's field, the chance of higher education—down to the mere possibility of living in that limited degree of legal certainty available to other citizens, instead of finding oneself amongst the special class to whom not even those laws which apply to the rest of the public apply, in other words, among the victims of Czech political apartheid. Yes, everyone has something to lose...

...I have made it clear that I have no fear of life in Czechoslovakia coming to a halt, or of history being suspended for ever with the accession to power of the present leaders. Every situation in history and every epoch have been succeeded by a fresh situation and a new epoch, and for better or worse, the new ones have always been quite remote from the expectat-ions of the organizers and rulers of the preceeding period.

What I am afraid of is something else. The whole of this letter is concerned, in fact, with what I really fear—the pointlessly harsh and long- lasting consequences which the present violent abuses will have for our nations. I fear the price we are all bound to pay for the drastic suppression of history, the cruel and needless banishment of life into the underground of society and the depths of the human soul, the new compulsory 'deferment' of every opportunity for society to live in anything like a natural way. And perhaps it is apparent from what I wrote a little way back that I am not only worried about our current payments in terms of everday bitterness at the spoliation of society and human degradation, or about the heavy tax we shall have to pay in the shape of a long-lasting spiritual and moral decline of society. I am also concerned with the scarcely calculable surcharge which may be imposed on us when the moment next arrives for life and history to demand their due.

The degree of reponsibility a political leader bears for the condition of his country must always vary and, obviously, can never be absolute. He never rules alone, and so some portion of responsibility rests on those who surround him. No country exists in a vacuum, so its policies are in some way always influenced by those of other countries. Clearly the previous rulers always have much to answer for, since it was their policies which predetermined the present situation. The public, too, has much to answer for, both individually, through the daily personal decisions of each responsible human being which went to create the total state of affairs, or collectively, as a socio-historic whole, limited by circumstances and in its turn limiting those circumstances.

Despite these qualifications, which naturally apply in our current situation as in any other, your responsibility as political leader is still a great one. You help to determine the climate in which we all have to live and can therfore directly influence the final size of the bill our society will be paying for today's process of 'consolidation'.

The Czechs and Slovaks, like any other nation, harbour within themselves simultaneously the most disparate potentialities. We have had, still have and will continue to have our heroes, and, equally, our informers and traitors. We are capable of unleashing our imagination and creativity, of rising spiritually and morally to unexpected heights, of fighting for the truth and sacrificing ourselves for others.

But it lies in us equally to succumb to total apathy, to take no interest in anything but our bellies and to spend our time tripping one another up. And though human souls are far from being mere pint pots that anything can be poured into (note the arrogant implications of that dreadful phrase so frequent in official speeches, when it is complained that 'we'—that is, 'the government'—find that such and such ideas are 'being instilled into people's heads'), it depends, nevertheless, very much on the leaders which of these contrary tendencies that slumber in society will be mobilized, which set of potentialities will be given the chance of fulfilment and which will be suppressed.

So far, it is the worst in us which is being systematically activated and

enlarged—egotism, hypocrisy, indifference, cowardice, fear, resignation and the desire to escape every personal responsibility, regardless of the general consequences.

Yet even today's national leadership has the opportunity to influence society by its policies in such a way as to encourage not the worst side of us, but the better.

So far, you and your government have chosen the easy way out for yourselves, and the most dangerous road for society: the path of inner decay for the sake of outward appearances; of deadening life for the sake of increasing uniformity; or deepening degrading human dignity for the puny sake of protecting your own power.

Yet, even within the given limitations, you have the chance to do much towards at least a relative improvement of the situation. This might be a *more strenuous and less gratifying way, whose benefits would not be immediately obvious and which would meet with resistance here and there. But in the light of our society's true interests and prospects, this way would be vastly the more meaningful one.*

As a citizen of this country, I hereby request, openly and publicly, that you and the leading representatives of the present regime consider seriously the matters to which I have tried to draw your attention, that you assess in their light the degree of your historic responsibility and act accordingly.

Excerpts from a letter to Dr Gustáv Husák, General Secretary of the Czechoslovak Communist Party, from Václav Havel, 8 April 1975. (Taken from Living in Truth, *Václav Havel, 1986.)*

Born in 1936, Václav Havel is Czechoslovakia's most important play-wright. An unrelenting critic of the Communist Party throughout his career, he endured imprisonment on more than one occasion. He was one of the founders of Charter 77, leading a bloodless revolution which saw him transformed from political dissident, to president-elect of his country.

Removal of communist slogans, December 1989 (left); flowers of peace, 21 August 1990 (above)

THE RULERS OF BOHEMIA

THE PŘEMYSLIDS

Wenceslas of Bohemia killed by brother Boleslav I	835
Boleslav II, Duke of Bohemia	967–999
Břatislav I, Duke of Bohemia	1034–1055
Vratislav I, King of Bohemia	1085–1092
Vladislav II	1140–1197
Otakar I	1197–1230
Wenceslas I	1230–1253
Otakar II	1253–1278
Wenceslas II	1278–1305
Wenceslas III	1305–1306

THE LUXEMBOURGS

John of Luxembourg	1310–1346
Charles IV of Luxembourg	1346–1378
Wenceslas IV	1378–1419
Sigismund	1419–1437 (Hussite War period)
Ladislav the Posthumous	1440–1458
George Poděbrady	452–1471 (regent, then King in 1458)

THE JAGIELLOS

Vladislav Jagiello	1471–1516
Ludvik II	1516–1526

THE HAPSBURGS

Ferdinand I	1526–1564
Maximilian II	1564–1576
Rudolf II	1576–1611 (abdicated)
Matthias	1612–1619
Frederick V	1619–1620 (the Winter King)
Ferdinand II	1620–1637
Ferdinand III	1637–1657
Ferdinand IV	1646–1654
Leopold I	1657–1705
Joseph I	1705–1711
Charles VI	1711–1740
Maria Theresa	1740–1780
Joseph II	1765–1790
Leopold II	1790–1792
Francis II (František)	1792–1835
Ferdinand V	1835–December 1848 (abdicated)
Franz Josef	1848–1916
Charles	1916–28 October 1918

Statue of Charles IV, built in 1848 to celebrate 500 years of the foundation of Charles University, Square of Knights of the Cross

Staré město—Old Town

Movement along the trade route crossing Bohemia began as early as the 10th century. Settlements and market places became especially popular in the area between Prague Castle and Vyšehrad. By the 11th century it was fairly well settled, with the beginnings of a sophisticated town. During the years 1232 to 1234, King Wenceslas I had the area fortified and constituted as a town. Today's main streets, Národní třída, Na příkopě and Revoluční follow along the lines of the early town fortifications. The name Na příkopě, means 'by the moat'. As with early castles, a moat was incorporated in the fortifications around Staré město, separating it from the sector called Nové město, or New Town.

Great development occurred in Prague all through the following period, known as the Přemyslid dynasty. During the 13th century Prague was elevated to one of the most important cities in central Europe. Quite literally so, as the section known as Staré město was originally some seven to nine feet below its present street level. Due to considerable flooding, the area gradually rose to its present level leaving many of the early Romanesque foundations hidden below street level.

The church where the first Utraquist communion took place in the 11th century, **St Martin in the Wall** (Kaple sv Martina), is tucked away in Martinská. The original Romanesque church, dating from 1178, the nave of which is preserved in the present church, served the needs of a village community that spread southwards in the direction of Nové město. The building is the earliest extant structure in the Vyšehrad and the oldest of Prague's three remaining rotundas.

These small churches were not a part of a unified town complex but stood rather as the focus of individual village communities. The real process of urbanization was restricted to the area around the **Old Town Square** (Staroměstké náměstí). Around that time there were twenty Romanesque rotundas of which only three have survived: one in the New Town, **Rotunda sv Longina** in Na Rybníčku; one at Vyšehrad, **St Martin's in the Wall** (Rotunda sv Martina); and one in Staré město, the **Rotunda of the Holy Cross** (Kaple sv kříže) in Karoliny Světlé.

The Romanesque settlements were surrounded by walls in 1231, when builders incorporated where possible the natural defensive opportunities afforded by the terrain. It was this inclusion in the fortification walls that gave the Church of St Martin in the Wall its unusual name in the English translation.

During the reign of Charles IV, Prague became the capital of the Holy Roman Empire and experienced enormous economic growth, and in 1338 the citizens of Staré město were granted the rights for their own town hall. Ten years later, **Charles University** (Univerzita Karlova), the oldest university in central Europe, was founded, firmly establishing Prague as a cultural centre as well.

Astronomical Clock, Old Town Hall, built c.1410 by Mikuláš of Kadaň

In 1784, the towns of Prague were united into a single administrative unit. Greater Prague was formed in 1920 by the incorporation of neighbouring communities and expansion to present day boundaries took place in 1974.

Prague's Old Town Square can be compared to the hub of a wheel with each of the streets leading off it as the spokes. No matter in which direction you decide to walk, you won't be disappointed.

Walking past the **House at the Minute** (Dům u Minuty) you will come to **Malé náměstí**, or Little Square, surrounded by many Romanesque ruins and ranks among the oldest spaces in the area. The fountain in the centre is decorated with Romanesque grillework wrought in 1560. The lion dates from the mid-17th century.

Though there are many breathtaking buildings on the square which have recently been restored, the best is Rott's with its richly decorated façade showing allegories of Craft and Agriculture. Two whole floors of the original Romanesque building have been preserved. In the 15th century, the house became a printing shop where the first Czech Bible was published in 1488. Today the building houses an ironmonger's, which makes an interesting comparison to your local DIY.

Also on Malé náměstí is the Gothic building now housing the American Hospitality Center. Established on 4 July 1990, to help the hordes of English speaking tourists, it has now become firmly entrenched in the local scene. You can buy American coffee, pizza and popcorn, pick up messages, send a fax, find a guide, buy T-shirts or just pass time.

Any direction you wander in from here is fascinating but, if time is limited, turn left out of the American Hospitality Center and follow the crowds strolling towards Karlova. Do not be surprised if one or two of the narrow twisting streets are blocked and fake snow is being blown from huge trucks for the filming of some new movie or commercial. Since the buildings have changed very little in centuries, only a change of costume is necessary to transport you into a different time period.

Once housing wealthy merchants and their shops, Karlova and its sidestreets are now filled with souvenir shops, wine bars and art galleries. Where the roads widen, you will find dozens of young men selling Russian soldiers' gear, caviar and whatever other trinkets they have managed to pick up. Just before the Klementinum you will see the **House at the Golden Serpent** (Dům u zlatého hada). It was in this Renaissance house, with its sign in the form of a golden snake, that an Armenian named Deodatus Damajan opened the first Prague coffee house in 1714. Now it is an excellent restaurant with fine local house wines.

Continuing toward Charles Bridge (Karlův most), you will come to the **Church of St Saviour**, which faces the Square of the Knights of the Cross (Křižovnické náměstí) and the Bridge Tower. The church is part of the vast **Klementinum**, a Jesuit complex spreading over two hectares. Inside are churches, gardens, rich stucco deco-

Old Town Square with the Church of our Lady before Týn c. 1920

rations, the Chapel of Mirrors, fine frescoes and unsurpassed sculpture. The eastern wing, facing Seminářská, contains a reading room and the State Technical Library. Just up the street is náměstí Primátora Dr Vacka, where the Municipal Popular Library is located. The late Art Nouveau building nearby is the **New Town Hall** (Novoměstská radnice), seat of the mayor of Prague and the National Committee.

In the nearby garden of the Baroque **Clam-Gallas Palace** (Clam-Gallasův palác), designed by Viennese court architect J B Fischer von Erlach, is a fountain with an allegorical sculpture of the Vltava by Prachner.

The **Convent of St Agnes** (Klášter sv Anežky České), called the Bohemian Assisi, was founded in 1233 by King Wenceslas I on the suggestion of his sister, Anežka of Bohemia, who introduced the Order of the Poor Clares, the female branch of the Franciscan Order, into Bohemia. During reconstruction in 1985 and 1986, archaeologists uncovered the skeletal remains of the king. The newly adapted interiors of the convent now serve as the National Gallery, offering exhibitions of early Czech painting. Concerts are held in the cloister.

Walk now toward **Betlémské náměstí**, Bethlehem Square, where **Bethlehem Chapel** (Betlémská kaple), built in 1391 to 1394, stands as an important memorial to the Hussite period and the Reformation movement. In the 17th and 18th centuries, the chapel was taken over by the Jesuits. After the abolition of their Order in 1773, the chapel was closed and subsequently demolished in 1786. The chapel that exists today is a faithful reconstruction of the original by architect Fragner, utilizing much of the original foundations. The work was completed in 1954 by the Czechoslovak government. Burial remains, the foundations of the original pillars and three metal-casting furnaces from the 11th century have been preserved in the cellarage, where the preacher's house is located. Both the chapel and the preacher's house have been declared national cultural monuments and are open to the public.

Next, stroll along the Vltava to Národní and Legion's Bridge (most Legii). where you will see the massive Neo-Renaissance structure of the **National Theatre** (Národní divadlo). This was built in the 1870s after a plan by Josef Zítek with funds gained through national collection after the people's request for a national theatre was turned down by the authorities. Just after completion in 1881, the building was completely destroyed by fire. Undaunted, the people of Prague donated their time and money a second time and the National Theatre was reopened with grand ceremony on 18 November 1883 under the direction of Josef Schulz. The five arcades of the loggia (facing Národní) are decorated with lunette paintings symbolizing the Five Songs and statues of Apollo and the Nine Muses by Bohuslav Schnirch. The bronze triga with the chariot of the Goddess of Victory on the pylons of the main façade was sculpted by Rous, Halman and Saloun. On the western side facing the embankment are statues representing Opera and Drama.

Flower market, Havelská, with the Church of St Gall in the background

Next door to the National Theatre is the seven storey steel skeleton of the **New Stage** (Nová Scéna), built between 1977–1983. If you can stand the reflected glare, there is a lovely open-air café in the garden.

Be sure to cross the street to the **Café Slávia**. Resident in the former **Lazanský Palace** for over a century, this is one of the last great coffee houses of central Europe. Arrive early and choose a window seat. The view both inside and out is well worth it!

Continuing toward Wenceslas Square (Václavské náměstí) you will pass the **Ursuline Convent** and the **Ursuline Church**. The renovated 17th-century buildings house various medical institutes and a fine wine bar and restaurant.

On the left is the Art Nouveau home of the Union of Czechoslovak Writers and **Bartolomějská**, headquarters of the former Secret Police.

A block further on you will come to **Máj Department Store**, one of the largest in Prague. Today it is hard to believe that the building you see before you stands on the ruins of vaulted Gothic cellars.

Platey's House (Dům u Platey), the interior of which is decorated with large painted frieze, is one of the oldest in the area and faces the former **Coal Market**. The Staré město fortifications and ditches originally stretched through this area and St Martin in the Wall (Kaple sv Martina) is nearby. The ceiling joists inside the house and the late Gothic stone pillar in the connecting passageway date from the 15th century. Between 1840–1846, Franz Liszt used to give concerts here. Today the house is the seat of the Czech Fund of Fine Arts.

Back on Národní, you reach the Venetian Renaissance **Adria Palace**, now home to the Film Club and the wonderful experimental theatre, **Laterna Magica**. On the terrace overlooking Národní is a superb wine bar which really comes alive in spring.

Another ancient market street, alley V kotcích, leads toward the **Fruit Market** and the **Karolinum**, the oldest university building still in use on the European continent. **Estates Theatre**, the oldest theatre in the city and stage of the world première of Mozart's *Don Giovanni* on 29 October 1787, lies between the fruit market and Želetná.

Crossing Wenceslas Square (Václavské náměstí) from Národní (just at the metro stop Můstek) is Prague's main shopping street, **Na příkopě**, which leads all the way up to Republican Square (Náměstí Republiky). Though many buildings are being taken over by modern design houses, this has been Prague's high fashion district for the last century. Be sure to take a look at Dům Elegance and the showrooms of Bohemia Crystal. You will also find the main banks located along this street (if you do not need to change money, go just to see the architecture) and the headquarters of Čedok. The **Sylva-Taroucca Palace** on the right is a fine example of Baroque architecture, as the original mythological sculptures and vases by Ignaz Franz Platzer are still on the pillars of the wrought iron balustrade. The palace now serves as a venue for cultural and social events and often organizes jazz evenings. Further up on the left is the Moscow Restaurant and Prague's answer to fast food, the Arbat.

At the end of Na příkopě you will be facing the late Gothic **Powder Tower** (Prašná brána), built in the second half of the 15th century, and the superb Art Nouveau **People's Municipal House** (Obecní dům). The Powder Tower was once the monumental entrance gate to Staré město. The original tower, Odrana, built in the first half of the 13th century, was connected to the fortification ditch. The new tower was founded in 1475 by King Vladislav Jagiello, although construction halted in 1484 when the king moved from the neighbouring royal court to Prague Castle. The unfinished tower was given a temporary roof and used to store gunpowder, hence its name. The tower is open to the public on Wednesdays and weekends from April to October.

The People's Municipal House stands on the site of the former royal court and was built by the community of Prague from 1906–1911. The construction plans were the work of Balšánek and Polívka but the six halls, restaurants and offices of the interior were designed by an entire generation of Czech artists. A fitting tribute occurred on 6 January 1918, when the Three Magi's Declaration of the Czechoslovak Republic was pronounced from this building. On 28 October, the independence of Czechoslovakia was proclaimed and the first law of the new republic issued. Weekly concerts and the Prague Spring Music Festival are held in the grand Smetana Hall (see Art Nouveau in Prague, page 140). In the basement is a wine cellar with colourful ceramic decorations after a design by Obrovský.

On 13 September 1920, the 13th Congress of the Social Democratic Party took place here, headed by Dr B Šmeral, who proclaimed support for the principles of the Communist Internationale, the first step towards the formation of the Czech Communist Party.

Just behind the Obecní dům is the lovely **Hotel Paříž**, credited as one of the finest examples of Viennese Secessionist style.

Walk through the Powder Tower and you will be in Čeletná, beginning of the **Royal Mile**, the route taken for centuries by the kings and queens of Bohemia on their way to coronations or to welcome festive arrivals in Staré město. It led from the Powder Tower, which in the Middle Ages stood next to the former royal town palace, up Čeletná, across Staré město and Malé náměstí, into winding Karlova and the square named after the Knights of the Cross, across Charles Bridge and Lesser Town Square (Malostranské náměstí), and then up Neruda to Prague Castle.

But first, take a wander back down **Čeletná** toward Old Town Square (Staroměstké náměstí). Named after the *calt*—the roll the bakers made here in the Middle Ages—this is one of the oldest streets in Prague. The cellar walls of some of these magnificently restored baroque houses date back to the 13th century.

The first building on the left is the old **Mint**, which was founded in 1420 during the Hussite Revolution. The mint moved around until 1783, when the present house was built to the order of the Master of the Mint, František Josef Pachta. In 1784, it was rebuilt as military headquarters, and in 1850 it was turned into court offices. The adjoining building, facing the Fruit Market, was built in neo-rococo style.

Just at the next corner is the **House at the Black Mother of God**, an outstanding representative of cubist architecture built in 1911–1912. The only reminder of the original early baroque house occupying this site is the 17th-century house sign **Our Lady Behind the Grille**. The entire street is an outdoor museum of house signs.

There are several fine wine cellars and restaurants along this street. At the **Manhart House** (No 17) is a picturesque garden with an early baroque statue of a woman as its centrepiece and a statue of Hercules in the arcade. Follow the ancient staircase down to the wine cellar **U pavouka**, or Spider. Nearby is **U zlatého jelena** (Golden Stag), a wonderful dining experience.

Halfway down the street is

Wooden figure from the Astronomical Clock, Old Town Hall

House at the Minute

the restaurant **U supa**, the Vulture. Just before you reach the Old Town Square is the restaurant **U Sixtů**, whose basement contains the well preserved barrel and cross vault remains of the original late Romanesque structure.

Some mention must be made of the absolutely delightful **Havelská**, which has been a market from the early 13th century. Wine can be bought straight from the barrel and fresh produce is on offer whenever it is available. The **Church of St Gall** is a Gothic creation built on the 13th-century foundations of the convent of the Magdalene Order. The houses along the street maintain their Gothic arcading with cross vaults and bolts, decorated with a relief rosette motif.

OLD TOWN SQUARE (STAROMĚSTSKÉ NÁMĚSTÍ)

■ **THE ROMANESQUE PERIOD**

There is a certain fairy-tale quality about the Old Town Square that makes it more like a stage setting than anything from real life. Whether you see it covered with the first dusting of powdery snow or brimming with open air cafés and spring flowers, it will take your breath away.

A square is always the focal point of local society, where all life comes together to exchange news, celebrate events or share mutual grief or excitement. The square is also considered the main marketplace and, in the 14th century, it was actually called the Great Marketplace or the Great Ring. By 1850 it had become the Great Square, and in 1895 it acquired its present name.

A 10th-century Arab traveller and diplomat wrote the first account of the city called Prague. Even at that time it was an important crossroads of merchant routes and a highly sophisticated marketplace. He described a large town built of stone and lime spread out below a grand castle.

There were many settlements in this area, divided according to nationalities. Germans, Jews and Romans existed side by side in the land along the Vltava. Though sparsely settled at first, the network of inhabited areas slowly began to spread. During the 12th century, under the reign of Prince Vladislav II, the appearance of the settlement changed significantly, and by the 13th century, the marketplace was already taking on the appearance of a town square.

Prince Vladislav was a traveller as well as a soldier in the army of Emperor Frederick Barbarossa. During his tour of Northern Italy and parts of Germany, he saw many varied architectural styles which had not been used in the settlements around Prague. Upon his return he initiated vast projects and the construction of stone houses commenced. The first stone bridge over the Vltava was built and named after Vladislav's wife Judith.

It was during this era that the present square acquired its general appearance. The remains of many 12th-century buildings have been imaginatively incorporated into basements: the restaurant U Sixtů is a good example.

For the most part, the living quarters of these Romanesque houses faced the street, forming the façade. At the centre of the house was a large hall surrounded by smaller rooms. The back part of the house was usually wooden and used for commercial purposes. The main entrances did not open directly onto the street but onto small passageways running between the houses.

The houses on the north, east and south sides of today's square correspond to the line of the Romanesque houses around the marketplace. Not much is known about the first owners, but reports suggest many were merchants of German origin.

The east side of the square, where the baroque Goltz-Kinský Palace (palác Kinských) stands, is early medieval. This was the site of the fortified Týn, where foreign merchants came to sell their goods, and where the King's Officer resided to ensure peace and order and to collect customs fees. He was the keeper of official weights and measures, which made him an essential part of the business community. This section also had a hospital and chapel.

The western side of the market place was larger than it is today, as it included the eastern part of the town hall and extended as far as the House at the Cockerel. The Church of St Nicholas (Kostel sv Mikuláše) was built on the northern edge of the marketplace, serving as a gathering place for the municipal community until the construction of the Old Town Hall (Staroměstská radnice).

■ THE GOTHIC PERIOD

By the 13th century, the transformation from a rural settlement into a real town was complete. Walls were built surrounding the area and new laws introduced to govern it as a community. A municipal council of aldermen was selected by the king and a Royal Officer installed.

As time passed the people gained more influence over the burghers. The wealth of the community grew as did the self-confidence of the local ruler. By the end of the 13th century a town office was established, guaranteeing town council independence from the magistrate, although most meetings continued to take place either at the house of the magistrate or at the Church of St Nicholas. Then in 1338, King John of Luxembourg approved the purchase of the house in the middle of the Ring, and the rebuilding of a town hall on that site. The Old Town Hall has since become a symbol of municipal self-government and, in order to preserve their independence, the burghers of Staré město passed a law by which anyone trying to usurp authority from the town, even those with the blessings of the king, would be tried.

When Holy Roman Emperor Charles IV chose Prague as his Imperial Residence in 1346, the city became the wealthiest in the Kingdom of Bohemia. The population swelled to over 40,000 strong, making it not only the largest, but the most densely populated city in central Europe.

Unfortunately, many of Charles IV's efforts to glorify Prague ceased with his death in 1378. Under Wenceslas IV, Prague slipped into a tremendous economic depression and, by the end of the 14th century, the deterioration of the economy had caused much social tension and severe criticism of the Church. In 1415, student Jan Hus was burned at the stake and in 1419, radical preacher Jan Želivský took the town hall by force and threw the aldermen out of the windows.

During this period, known as the Hussite Wars after the followers of Jan Hus, Prague burghers confiscated many properties from the Church and from wealthy German patricians. Rebellions occurred, both against the radical Hussites and the government. In 1437, the people built a giant gallows on Old Town Square (Staroměstské náměstí) and the last of the Hussite captains, Jan Roháč, and 60 of his warriors were executed.

Bohemian nobility were the real winners of the Hussite Wars. During the decade from 1430–40, the Catholic city governors were expelled and Prague's independence legally confirmed. By the end of the decade, Prague had become the head of the royal towns and seat of the new Reformed Church and the university. The new provincial parliament was elected by the people and met regularly in the town hall.

> 'They bid ring the bells from the towers on high,
> And the folk all flocked to the Týn hard by;
> Not long did the priests in the church there stay,
> But streamed to the Ring in the light of day.
> And they cried aloud with fearful cries:
> "Beloved, we're threatened! To arms! Arise!"
> And the streaming folk then quickly knew,
> With treacherous letters they had to do.'   German, 15th century

The Old Town Hall had become so important that in 1458 it was selected as the site for the election of the new king, Jiří of Poděbrady. In recognition of the town hall's new status, the Prague coat-of-arms was granted an improvement in 1475. The silver town hall was replaced with one of gold and a plumed helmet and imperial crown were added with a double-tailed lion on either side. This coat-of-arms is still the basis of the emblem for Staré město, and gold and red have become the official Prague colours.

During the Gothic period architecture around Staroměstské náměstí changed significantly, most notably shown in the town hall complex and the churches of St Nicholas (Kostel sv Mikuláše) and Our Lady before Týn (Týnsky chram). Burghers' houses constructed around the public building complex vastly increased in size. With improved public safety, the entrances began to face the main streets and the houses grew closer together. Another characteristic sign of this period are the vaulted arcades that expanded the living space of the upper stories and provided shelter to pedestrians. The oldest arcade is preserved in the house by the Týn School.

During the 14th and 15th centuries, the burgher class became all important and their homes were decorated to complement their status. These houses were characterized by two halls, one above the other, with vaulted ceilings and a connecting passageway to the ground floor courtyard. The lower hall was used for commercial purposes, the upper hall served as an elegant living space for the owner's family.

The House at the Golden Unicorn (U zlatého jednorožce), on the corner of Železná and Old Town Square, shows the remains of a vaulted passageway and part of the main entrance portal of a home built at the end of the 15th century by a famed Prague stonemason, Matěj Rejsek. The House at the Stone Bell (Dům u kamenného zvonu), one of several occupied by members of the ruling family, is another notable home from the Gothic period.

It was from this time that the now famous Prague house signs first appeared. The town had become so densely populated with fine homes that it was easy for the visitor to become confused. Elaborate stone or wooden sculptures with painstakingly painted designs were incorporated into the space above the main entrance. Even in the 15th century, house signs were used in municipal records for the identification of individual houses as surnames were still not commonplace.

■ THE RENAISSANCE PERIOD

By the Treaty of Brussels (1522), Holy Roman Emperor Charles V assigned the Hapsburg-Austrian possessions to his brother Ferdinand, who was crowned King of Bohemia in 1526. This was not beneficial to the Bohemians, as Ferdinand brought to the throne much stricter centralism and state power. The burghers were forced into subservience and uprisings occurred. At Ferdinand's insistence, the Jesuits came to Prague and, in 1561, the archbishopric was renewed.

Old Town Hall c. 1940

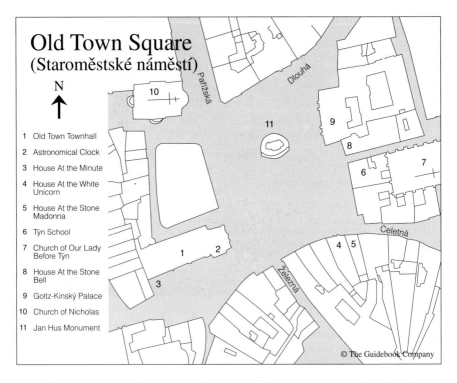

Old Town Square
(Staroměstské náměstí)

N ↑

1 Old Town Townhall

2 Astronomical Clock

3 House At the Minute

4 House At the White Unicorn

5 House At the Stone Madonna

6 Týn School

7 Church of Our Lady Before Týn

8 House At the Stone Bell

9 Goltz-Kinský Palace

10 Church of Nicholas

11 Jan Hus Monument

© The Guidebook Company

The Renaissance style first arrived in Prague with the construction of Ferdinand I's pleasure palace, the Royal Summer Palace, which became a model for other palaces. However, as most building activity was confined to court circles, little new construction took place on the square. Any change that did occur was in the form of renovation, especially to the Gothic façades and gables. Richly decorated windows were added to the Old Town Hall. Týn School was completed during this period, as were some outstanding renovations to the House at the Stone Ram, where old style gables gave way to the typical rising gables. The House at the Minute (Dům u minuty), whose sgrafitto façade was added in two phases during the 17th century, later became part of the complex of the Old Town Hall.

■ THE BAROQUE PERIOD

A period of sluggish development ended when Emperor Rudolf II ascended the throne, moving his entire court and administration to Prague. The glamour brought by the imperial court made Prague the centre of both political events and the arts.

This time of glory was short lived, however, as Rudolf's heir was to abandon

Prague forever in favour of a court in Vienna. The religious conflicts, which had ebbed, returned in far greater volume. Uprisings and executions occurred, complicated further by the onset of the Thirty Years' War and the Swedish attempt to invade Prague.

After the Hapsburg victory over the Swedes at the Battle of White Mountain, ending the Thirty Years' War, Catholicism became firmly entrenched in Prague, bringing with it the new baroque style. Both the Church and the new nobility acquired extensive property in town through confiscation from former Swedish owners, creating ideal conditions for the propagation of baroque architecture. Baroque stucco façades changed the appearance of whole neighbourhoods and the proliferation of baroque church towers drew a new skyline. The façades along the south side of the square are some of the best preserved examples of the era in central Europe.

Though the original baroque pillar by Jan Jiří Bendl was later destroyed, one magnificent monument remains—the **Goltz-Kinský Palace** (palác Kinských) built in 1755–1765. It is richly decorated with rococo stucco overlays and ornate gables. On the northwest corner of the square are the baroque remains of the former monastery of the Paulans. The Church of St Nicholas (Kostel sv Mikuláše), though not originally intended as part of the square, is a fine baroque addition.

■ THE MODERN AGE

The primary change to occur in the square during the 19th century was the demolition of the north wing of the Old Town Hall and the construction of its neo-Gothic replacement. With the subsequent (1893–1901) demolition of the old Jewish ghetto, the entire north front of the square was affected. Beautiful sweeping streets leading off the square, such as **Pařížská**, were created giving rise to one of Prague's most notable architectural styles, Art Nouveau.

In 1898, the **Palace of the Prague Insurance Company** was built on the north side of the square. The **Monument to Jan Hus**, arguably one of the city's most famous statues, was added in 1915.

Although most of Prague has been miraculously saved from wartime destruction, fighting during World War II set fire to the northern wing of the Old Town Hall. This section was removed and replaced with a small temporary park area. A plaque on the back wall of the town hall tells of the destruction. Numerous competitions to select a replacement design for the wing have been held, but none so far have met with widespread approval.

Since the fire there have been no major changes to the permanent structure of the square. For the last 40 years, at Christmas, Čedok has erected a tree and various stalls appear selling local crafts. In spring, open-air wine bars are now *de rigueur* and are an excellent place to sit back and soak in the atmosphere.

OLD TOWN HALL (STAROMĚSTSKÁ RADNICE)

Probably the most popular building in Prague, for locals and visitors alike, is the **Old Town Hall**. Not only is it the administration centre, but the centre of Prague as well. The building originated on the basis of a privilege granted by King John of Luxembourg on 18 September 1338. In that year the community purchased the Early Gothic house of Wolflin of Kamen and adapted it as the town hall. A second storey was added, a tower raised and after 1348, the citizens of Prague built a chapel on the first floor. Completed in 1381, when the richly decorated oriel window was added, the chapel today is the most popular place in Prague for weddings.

During the time of the Hussite uprisings, construction on the town hall came to a halt. Renovation did not begin again until the 15th and 16th centuries, when the block was changed to reflect the Late Gothic style.

The community acquired one of the neighbouring burgher's homes in 1458, that of the wealthy **Mikeš the Furrier**. Sometime during the previous 50 years, vaulted arcades had been added to the home, connecting it to a lane that led to the old goose market. Work on incorporating this house into the town hall complex lasted until 1470. Considerable changes were made to the façades of the individual buildings and their interiors, including the addition of a main portal and the window in the entrance hall. The portal is richly decorated with carved figural and vegetable motifs and in the window are emblems of Bohemia and Staré město. The most significant sculptural monument is that in the Old Council Hall of *Christ in Suffering*, dating from around 1400.

Around 1410, Mikuláš of Kadaň was commissioned to build the **Astronomical Clock**, which was perfected some eighty years later by Hanuš of Růže. During the 1500s, ornate carvings with a series of animal and plant motifs were added.

In the early 16th century changes were made in the layout of the first floor of the central house. A large and very beautiful Early Renaissance window bearing the inscription 'Praga caput regni', meaning 'Prague, head of the Kingdom', was built. In 1731 the window was enlarged with the addition of side windows and a grille.

Old Town Hall door detail

Looking north to the Monument to Jan Hus and Goltz-Kinský Palace from the Old Town Hall Tower

CHARLES BRIDGE

It is hard to recall Charles Bridge as it was back in the pre-Revolution days when a trickle of tourists arrived only briefly in summer. It is still a magical place but times have changed. Squashed cheek by jowl with 12th-century memories are street musicians, craftspeople, transient students, boys selling Soviet army gear, wine and cigarette vendors, mime artists and plenty of tourists.

The first small wooden bridge to cross the Vltava, situated slightly lower downriver, was mentioned in the 10th century. Around 1158, it was re-placed by a stone bridge built by King Vladislav in celebration of his coro-nation. The bridge was modelled on Europe's oldest stone bridge in Re-gensberg. As Vladislav travelled extensively, he was unable to supervise the construction personally and left the job in the capable hands of his second wife, Judith, after whom the bridge was later named. Judith Bridge was lower than, but ran almost parallel to, the present bridge until it was de-stroyed by flood in 1342. The Lesser Quarter bases correspond exactly.

The replacement bridge was commissioned by Emperor Charles IV, who laid the foundation stone on 9 July 1357, the day of Saturn's conjunction with the sun. The design, by world-renowned cathedral architect Petr Parléř, took over 50 years to complete, by which time Charles was already dead. It was not until 1870 that the bridge officially acquired his name.

The basic bridge is red and greenish sandstone, hewn into huge blocks. According to legend, wine and eggs were added to the mortar to make it stronger. As there were not enough eggs in Prague, all the towns of Moravia and Bohemia were required to contribute. Apparently the instructions were not always understood: some towns sent cheese and curd for good measure and the thoughtful town of Velvary hard-boiled all their eggs so they would not be broken in transit.

Most of the bridge is 7.5 metres (25 feet) wide though there are sections where it spans more than 10 metres (33 feet). The graceful semi-circular vaulted arches are supported by 16 piers. Both ends used to be protected by towers and gates, where a toll was collected in the 14th century.

This grandiose bridge became the main thoroughfare of town life. Not only did tradesmen cross and congregate here, but courts of judgement were convened and tournaments were held. According to hearsay, early forms of public punishment for dishonest tradesmen took the form of

Statues on Charles Bridge looking west to Hradčany, c. 1940

public dunkings in wicker baskets swung from the bridge. It was also part of the Royal Mile, the scene of Swedish invasions and a means of escape for the royal family.

The 30 sculptures now adorning the bridge did not come about all at once, nor did all the originals survive. The idea stemmed from Rome's Angel Bridge, but it was not until the 17th century that the first sculpture, that of John Nepomuk, was erected. It was rumoured that Nepomuk, the Vicar General, was tossed from the bridge on 20 March 1393, when he refused to reveal the secrets of Queen Sophia's confession to the king. Later history revealed the drowning took place because he confirmed the installation of the new Abbot of Kladruby Abbey against the wishes of the king.

The contrast between the Gothic architectural structure and the baroque sculptural groups lends the bridge much of its charm. Between 1706 and 1714 the bridge was adorned with 26 sculptures and groups of statues. Further work was not completed until the second half of the 19th century, when its famous appearance emerged. Last to be placed on the bridge were the statues of saints Cyril and Method by Dvořák in 1938. Gradually, however, the original sculptures are being transferred to the Municipal Gallery and replaced with replicas.

The Malá strana bridge tower has been preserved and incorporated into the **Monastery of the Knights of the Cross**. In the Staré město bridge tower much of Parléř's distinctive marbled brush work is visible. The elegant prismatoid tower ends in a gallery and battlement with four corner turrets. A wedge-shaped roof is topped by two golden globes and discs of the sun.

Statue of St John Nepomuk, Charles Bridge

Prominently positioned is the spread eagle, emblem of the Holy Roman Empire. On the right the Czech lion commands the place of honour, followed by the town crests of Zhorelec, Budysín and Dolní Luzice.

On the battlement above the broken arches are copies of the ten coats of arms belonging to the lands of the Czech Kingdom. For military reasons the passageway was not vaulted, allowing the defenders to strike their attackers from the galleries on the first floor. This is where the original coats of arms are found.

During reconstruction in 1874–1880, a wooden neo-Gothic panelled ceiling was fitted on the second floor of the Old Town bridge tower. At that time the archway frescoes were repainted and the Prague coat of arms added.

At the end of the bridge on the left-hand side (in front of the Malá strana bridge towers), is a 1591 Renaissance house which once served as the toll house. On the first floor is a rare Romanesque relief from the mid-13th century, originally part of the bridge façade decoration.

Over the centuries traffic on the bridge became heavier and heavier causing serious structural problems. Probably the greatest injustice was the car and tram traffic which passed over the bridge until the mid-1970s. In 1974 the last reconstruction project was completed leaving the bridge more or less in peace as the most magical promenade in central Europe.

Further notes on the statues:
2) **The Holy Saviour and Saints Cosmos and Damian** was donated by the medical faculty of Charles University, as the clothing of the two saints shows.

Statue of Christ (J Mayer, 1709), Charles Bridge

Charles' Bridge Statues

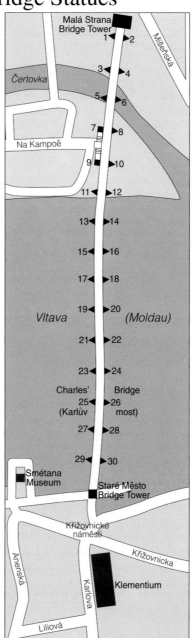

Malá Strana
Bridge Tower

Čertovka

Na Kampoě

Vltava

(Moldau)

Charles'   Bridge

(Karlův   most)

Smétana
Museum

Staré Město
Bridge Tower

Křižovnické
náměstí

Křižovnická

Anenská

Karlova

Liliová

Klementium

1 St Wenceslas,
   J K Bohm,1858.

3 Saints John de Matha,
   Felix de Valois and
   Ivan, F M Brokoff,1714.

5 St Aldalbert,
   J M Brokoff,1709,
   copy by Hořínek, 1973.

7 St Luitgarde,
   M B Braun, 1710.

9 St Nicholas of
   Tolentino, J B Kohl,
   1708.

11 St Vincent Ferrarius
   and St Procopius,
   F M Brokoff, 1712.

13 St Francis of Assisi,
   E Max, 1855.

15 Saints Ludmila and
   Wenceslas, M B Braun,
   1720.

17 St Francis Borgia,
   F M Brokoff, 1710.

19 St Christopher, E Max,
   1857.

21 St Francis Xavier, F M
   Brokoff, 1711, copy
   Čeněk Vosmík, 1913.

23 St Joseph, J Max,
   1854.

25 Pieta, E Max, 1859.

27 Saints Barbara,
   Margaret and
   Elizabeth, F M Brokoff,
   1707.

29 St Ives, M B Braun,
   1711, copy by
   J Hergesel, 1908.

2 The Holy Saviour and
   Saints Cosmas and
   Damian, J O Mayer,
   1709.

4 St Vitus, F M Brokoff,
   1714.

6 St Philip Benitius,
   M B Mandl, 1714.

8 St Theatin,
   F M Brokoff, 1709.

10 St Augustine,
   J B Kohl, 1708.

12 St Jude Thaddeus,
   J O Mayer, 1708.

14 St Anthony of Padua,
   J O Mayer, 1707.

16 St John Nepomuk,
   J Brokoff, 1683.

18 Saints Norbert,
   Wenceslas and
   Sigismund, J Max,
   1853.

20 St John the Baptist,
   J Max, 1857.

22 Saints Cyril and
   Method, K Dvořák,
   1938.

24 St Anne, M V Jackel,
   1707.

26 Calvary—A Group of
   Statues with the Holy
   Cross, E Max, 1861.

28 The Madonna and
   Saints Dominic and
   Thomas Aquinus, M V
   Jackel, 1708, copy by
   F Bartůněk, 1965.

30 The Madonna and St
   Bernard, M V Jackel,
   1709.

3) **Saints John de Matha, Felix de Valois and Ivan** This group of statues was set up by Count Thun in honour of the Trinitarian Order which ransomed Christians from Turkish captivity. The work depicts a Turk with a dog guarding a jail in which Christians are suffering. Standing above is St Ivan and the founders of the Order, John de Matha and Felix de Valois.

5) **St Aldalbert**, the second bishop of Prague.

6) **St Philip Benitius** Notice the papal crown, which he declined in 1268, at his feet. This is the only work sculpted in marble.

7) **St Luitgarde** This statue of the blind Cistercian nun is considered the most valuable and well exucuted of all the bridge statues.

11) **St Vincent Ferrarius and St Procopius** Note the inscription below the statue giving the list of St Vincent's converts.

12) **St Jude Thaddeus**, patron saint of troubled souls.

16) **St John Nepomuk**, the oldest statue on the bridge and the only one cast in bronze, was placed here by the Jesuit Order before he was canonized.

18) **Saints Norbert, Wenceslas and Sigismund**, J Max, 1853.

21) **St Francis Xavier**, a Jesuit missionary

22) **Saints Cyril and Method**, who brought Christianity to the Slavic peoples in the ninth century. Originally a statue of St Ignatius of Loyola by F M Brokoff stood here, but it collapsed into the Vltava during the flood of 1890.

23) **St Joseph**, a replacement of the original statue destroyed during the revolution of 1848.

26) **Calvary—A Group of Statues with the Holy Cross** was the first statue on the bridge and dates from the first half of the 17th century. It is placed where a Gothic cross stood as early as the 14th century. The Hebrew inscription on the cross, dating from 1696, was paid for from a fine imposed on a Jew who had mocked the cross.

The Language of Soup

Veronika's kitchen window looks out on to the backyard. It is in the old part of Prague—Staré Mjesto—where the houses look like fortresses, with strong walls and small windows. The façade across from her is crumbling from damp. The window is wet with raindrops. In the semi-darkness of the kitchen, Veronika moves silently, slowly. She doesn't have to tell me anything—her story, I mean. I can easily read it in her attitude, her movements, her absentminded glancing look, and her silence. She is making farina dumplings for the beef soup: one whole egg, a pinch of salt, a little oil, and a cup of farina. She mixes it automatically (the secret of good dumplings is in the mixing); there is no need to concentrate on her movements, this is what she does every Saturday. Nobody is home, her two sons are out, her husband Jiri, too. I know it's him that she is thinking about—his absence, longer and longer every day. She doesn't want him to leave, even if she knows he has a lover.

She doesn't have time during the week to cook; the kids eat at school, she and Jiri too. So on Saturday she goes to the open market and buys food, fresh meat or fish, maybe vegetables, depending on what there is to buy. Today she found kiwi for dessert. It was very expensive, but she bought it because it is Saturday and they will all eat together. For Saturday lunch she cooks meals that the kids like, that he likes . . . as if she is mixing some kind of magic potion that will keep her family together—at least for a while, at least around the table. It takes a long time for the soup to cook, but finally she speaks to me. 'It's just that he is so unhappy, so frustrated. I understand him. In such a system I am happy to work as a little bureaucrat. But he is a journalist, and you know what kind of pressure they suffer. I don't know how I can help him—or us. Because if he leaves us, I feel like everything will fall apart, even these thick walls around me.' After the long silence, her words fall heavily, like the drops of rain outside.

Slavenka Drakulić,
How We Survived Communism And Even Laughed, 1987

Slavenka Drakulić was born in Rijeka in 1949. An accomplished journalist, she is a regular contributor to international publications and is an active international feminist. She has received honours from several US universities, including a Fulbright Fellowship for writers.

The Old Town Hall kept its Gothic appearance until the 17th century, when more modifications were needed to accommodate its new uses. Between 1838 and 1848, the entire east wing was pulled down and replaced by a Romantic Gothic wing designed by Peter Nobile and Paul Sprenger. Eventually the **House at the Sign of the Cockerel** (1835) and **House at the Minute** (1896) were added.

During the Prague Uprising on 8 May 1945, the new wing was destroyed during a Nazi attack. Only a fragment of the masonry by the tower has been preserved. In its place, a park has been laid out while competitions go on to determine the design of a replacement wing.

The most obvious highlight of the town hall is its 15th-century **Astronomical Clock**. A morbid legend relates how Wenceslas IV (1378–1419) had the builder, Mikuláš of Kadaň, blinded so that his remarkable feat of engineering could never be repeated.

The clock consists of three sections. In the middle is the actual clock, which also shows the movement of the sun and moon through the zodiac. At the top are the mechanical figures and at the bottom is a calendar dial with signs of the zodiac and scenes from country life.

By far the most exciting spectacle in Prague occurs every hour on the hour. After each full hour has been struck, the figures of Christ and the twelve Apostles move past the two small windows under the roof. Between the windows is the figure of an angel. The statue of the skeleton, representing Death, pulls the rope of the bell, turns the hourglass and nods to the Turk standing beside him that his time has run out. The Turk shakes his head in denial, as do the statues of Vanity and the Miser at the opposite side. Finally the cock crows as the windows shut and the crowd gathered below usually gives out a cheer and applause.

Although the complicated clock shows the three time systems used in the Middle Ages, none of them are accurate enough to set your watch by, so two modern clocks have been added on the sides.

The calendar dial indicates the months in pictures. The day, its position in the week, month and year are shown, along with the phase of the moon and signs of the zodiac.

After watching the clock in action, be sure to enter the building for the guided tour which lasts around half an hour. The sumptuous halls are definitely worth seeing, though the clock mechanism is strictly off limits.

HOUSE AT THE MINUTE

Next door to the town hall is the marvellous sgraffito-covered **House at the Minute** (Dům u minuty). This visual delight was discovered in 1919 under layers of plaster. The original work on biblical and mythological themes was created by an unknown

(preceding page) Rott's House, 1890 décor, originally built in the 12th century

artist in the 17th century. The statue of a lion perched in a corner niche was added in the 18th century.

GOLTZ-KINSKÝ PALACE

Occupying the north-east edge of the square is the most beautiful rococo building in Prague, the National Gallery, formerly **Goltz-Kinský Palace** (palác Kinských). It was built in the years 1755–1765, in late baroque style after plans by Anselmo Lurago. In the basement of the palace are the preserved foundations of Romanesque dwellings. The palace now houses a collection of graphic art and often has interesting special exhibits. Next door, the **House at the Stone Bell** (U zvonu) is the result of costly reconstruction over the last two decades, during which the preserved Gothic front of a mid-14th century house was discovered under a 19th-century façade. The interior revealed a chapel and wall paintings from the same period. It is the only house in Prague to have been discovered in its original Gothic state. Its corner house-sign, a stone bell, may have been walled into the corner of the house in memory of events which took place in 1310, when John of Luxembourg marched his troops to Prague to retake the city from his enemies. The signal to attack was given by ringing a bell in Týn Church (Týnsky chram). Today the house serves the exhibition and cultural purposes of the Prague Gallery.

The arcades along this eastern side of the square are not all from the same period, as some of them were built after 1330, while the section with steeper vaulting is from the 13th century.

The **Church of Our Lady before Týn** is an outstanding example of a Gothic triple-nave church, founded in 1365 on the site of a Romanesque and early 12th-century Gothic church. The multi-turreted twin towers are 80 metres (262 feet) tall. If you enter the nave by the north portal you will see one of the most richly decorated entrances in the country. Of especial note in the interior are the Gothic pulpit, the Gothic Madonna, the oldest surviving tin baptismal font in Prague and a wealth of baroque paintings.

Of cultural interest, especially to astronomy buffs, is the relief and tomb of Danish astronomer Tycho Brahe. Brahe served as court astronomer under Rudolph II and was an early proponent of the theory of the sun orbiting the earth.

The baroque **Church of St Nicholas** (Kostel sv Mikuláše) dominates the northern corner of Old Town Square. Founded in the early 13th century by German merchants, the original building served as a gathering place for the entire community until the completion of Týn Church. The masterful plans for the present building, dating from 1732, were the work of Kilian Ignaz Dientzenhofer. Sculptures by Antonin Braun decorate the south façade which contains the main portal and two steeples. Bernard Spineti created the rich stucco decoration on the interior walls.

In the latter half of the 19th century, clearing of the Jewish ghetto was initiated to allow for the creation of Pařížská, which runs along the side of the church. During construction, Kren's House, which originally closed the northwest side of the square, was demolished. It is to Dienztenhofer's credit that the Church of St Nicholas was designed with the assumption that the onlooker would have no space from which to view the building.

The only remainder of the original architecture on the northern side of the square is the former Pauline monastery, **Klášter Paulanů**. An early baroque building, it was erected after 1684 and later connected by a roofed passageway with the Church of St Saviour.

Although the charming houses on the south side of the square are beautifully preserved with baroque façades, they are actually of Gothic origin.

One of the oldest Prague house signs can be seen at No 551-1 on Old Town Square. In the 15th century, the house, which has Romanesque masonry preserved in the basement, was known as the **House at the Stone Ram**. Since the 18th century, it has also been called the House at the White Unicorn (Dům u bílého jednorožce). Take a walk past and make your own interpretation.

The **House at the Stone Madonna**, built in 1897, is a neo-Renaissance replacement on Gothic ruins. Now known as the **Storch House** after its former publishing owners, it is famed for its elaborately painted Mikolas Aleš façade. The painting represents St Wenceslas on horseback as Prince and Protector of the Czech lands.

One house which might go overlooked but is worth a visit for the wine bar is the **House at the Green Frog** (Dům u zelené áby). It is tucked slightly to the rear of the small park behind Old Town Hall. Originally an early Gothic house, it was subjected to many reconstructions and remainders of the first periods are preserved in the basement. Be sure to have someone point out the chair that belonged to Mydlář the Executioner.

Last but not least, some mention must be made of Prague's most famous monument, the **Memorial to Jan Hus**, in the middle of the square. The creation of sculptor Ladislav Saloun, it was unveiled in 1915 to commemorate the 500th anniversary of Hus' death at the stake. Today it is Prague's most popular meeting place as the wide stairs and comfortable benches are the best place in town to sit, and sooner or later everyone will walk past.

St Nicholas Church, Old Town Square, c. 1940

Sunset

Slowly the west reaches for clothes of new colours
which it passes to a row of ancient trees.
You look, and soon these two worlds both leave you,
one part climbs toward heaven, one sinks to earth,

leaving you, not really belonging to either,
not so hopelessly dark as that house that is silent,
not so unswervingly given to the eternal as that thing
that turns to a star each night and climbs—

leaving you (it is impossible to untangle the threads)
your own life, timid and standing high and growing,
so that, sometimes blocked in, sometimes reaching out,
one moment your life is a stone in you, and the next, a star.

Rainer Maria Rilke,
from The Book of Pictures (Das Buch der Bilder), *1902–06*

The Solitary Person

Among so many people cozy in their homes,
I am like a man who explores far-off oceans.
Days with full stomachs stand on their tables;
I see a distant land full of images.

I sense another world close to me,
perhaps no more lived in than the moon;
they, however, never let a feeling alone,
and all the words they use are so worn.

The living things I brought back with me
hardly peep out, compared with all they own.
In their native country they were wild;
here they hold their breath from shame.

Rainer Maria Rilke,
from The Book of Pictures (Das Buch der Bilder), 1902–06

Rainer Maria Rilke, a native of Prague who wrote all his work in German, achieves in this collection of poems a fusion between the techniques of writing and painting.

Nové město—New Town

Nové město—a misleading term indeed—was founded by Charles IV in 1348 to provide extra space for Prague's rapidly growing population, especially the increasing number of artisans and craftsmen. Its fortifications, completed in 1350, covered nearly three kilometres sloping down from Karlov to Vyšehrad and over to the Botič. From the outset it was the largest of Prague's towns and housed the greatest number of poor.

The filling of the individual marketplaces and streets was determined by committee. Legal regulations and standards concerning the construction work as a whole were issued, along with specifications for the material to be used. This conception represents the biggest and most outstanding town planning work in medieval Europe. Though many attempts were made over the years to join up Nové město and Staré město, they all proved unsuccessful until 1784, when Nové město's autonomy was abolished and it was merged with the other towns of Prague to form a single municipal entity.

From the 18th century onwards, Nové město gradually became the financial, administrative and social centre of Prague. The commercial heart was concentrated around its gigantic Horse Market, the present day **Wenceslas Square** (Václavské náměstí), which acquired its present name in 1848. Though the imposing square, with its shops, restaurants, hotels and lively clubs, is actually a massive gardened boulevard 680 metres (744 yards) long and 60 metres (66 yards) wide, it shows nothing of its Gothic beginnings and has remained the pulse of the city. It is also the centre for most of Prague's petty crime, pick pockets, money changers and prostitutes.

Prague's most beloved statue, that of **St Wenceslas**, was erected in 1912 after 30 years of plans and designs by Josef Myslbek. It represents St Wenceslas on horseback with sculptures of Czech patron saints at his feet. In the foreground are Ludmila and Procopius with Agnes and Adalbert at the rear. The statue remains the focal point of Prague, a place where people congregate, announcements are made and demonstrations begin.

Wenceslas Square is crowned by the massive yet dramatic structure of the neo-Renaissance **National Museum** (Národní muzeum) built in the years 1885 to 1890 after the designs of Josef Schultz. Its façade, hall, staircase and ramp are decorated with sculptures by leading artists Wagner and Maudr. The museum houses vast historical and natural history exhibitions, as well as a library containing almost one million volumes and outstanding medieval manuscripts.

Shrine on the pavement in honour of Jan Palach, who burned himself to death in protest of the Soviet occupation, 16 January 1969

Grand Hotel Europa, Wenceslas Square, designed by Bedřich Bendelmayer in 1903

Though most of the baroque buildings that once graced the square have disappeared, a few of the remaining Art Nouveau façades are worth attention. The fabulous **Hotel Evropa**, conceived by Bendelmayer, Dryak and Hypsman, is unsurpassed in the purity of its design. Make sure to visit the charming coffee shop with its slightly off-key quartet—and outrageously expensive coffee—and take a look at the stained glass in the restaurant.

On the opposite side of the square is another Art Nouveau creation, the **Lucerna Palace**, built in 1912 by members of President Havel's family. Inside the building and leading to Štěpánská and Vodičkova is a passageway lined with shops, a cinema, a buffet and the Rokoko Theatre. Downstairs is a large hall where fancy balls and concerts are held and which was the site of forbidden underground concerts. Upstairs are the new offices of Prague's Playboy Magazine.

Though Jindřišská to the right has several fine Gothic buildings, such as the **Church of St Henry** and the **Belfry**, you will probably have more need for the **Main Post Office** (Hlavní pošta), once a large botanical garden. It is worth seeing for its unusual court type hall decorated in the 19th century with allegorical paintings referring to Postal Communication and Transport.

At the top of the square to the left of the National Museum is the **New Parliament Building**, a controversial glass structure replacing the old Produce Exchange. Just beyond is the 1888 Viennese-designed **Smetana Theatre**, built for the German population of the city. The interior is richly decorated with stuccowork by Strictius and paintings by Veith. Surrounded by such opulent beauty it is hard to imagine, unless you visited in the pre-Revolution days, the red star which hung garishly above the stage. You can also visit the **Smetana Museum** near Charles Bridge.

Josef Fanta was the designer of the Art Nouveau **Main Railway Station** (Hlavní nádraží). Built between 1901 and 1909, it is famous for its golden butterfly, its classic lines and, less attractively, its high crime rate.

(preceding pages) *Wenceslas Square from the National Museum c. 1940*

At the lower end of Wenceslas Square is the metro station Můstek, where the remains of the medieval bridge that once led to Staré město can be seen below ground. A small arcade cuts through into the Art Nouveau haven of Jungmann Square (Jungmannovo náměstí) where the church of St Mary of the Snows (Kostel Panny Marie Sněžné) once stood. Planned in 1347 as a massive monastic church for the royal coronation, funds were never forthcoming and all that remains is the choir. The 16th-century altar and font dating from 1459 are worth viewing and the solitude of the area is quite refreshing.

Smetana Museum, south of Charles Bridge

Along the former Gottwald Embankment is the characterless **Máneš Building** designed by Otakar Novotný in 1930 on the site of the Sitka Mills. This was the seat of the Máneš society of creative artists and today hosts some very fine exhibitions. There is also a pleasant restaurant with an observation terrace overlooking the Vltava. The original **Sitek Waterworks Tower** still stands in direct contrast to the next-door gallery. It was built in 1494, reconstructed in 1591, and once again in 1648.

Charles Square (Karlovo náměstí) was Nové město's main public gathering spot and the largest market since the time of Nové město's foundation in 1348. Called the Cattle Market until 1848, the area has remained very much like a large village green, and only a few seedier elements now gather at night. Emperor Charles IV had a wooden tower built here to display the imperial coronation jewels each year. The tower of the **Town Hall**, the Church of St Ignatius and Faustus House are the only original buildings to survive.

At the northern end of the square is the **New Town Hall** (Novoměstská radnice), founded before 1367. The two naves on the ground floor, now a cherished wedding hall, and the cellars have been preserved in their Gothic state. This was the site of the first Defenestration of Prague in 1419, when the Hussites, led by Jan Želivský, hurled the Catholic councillors from the windows, thus initiating the Hussite Wars. After

Passive Resistance

The commission of medical experts, which had to decide whether Švejk's mental horizon did or did not correspond to all the crimes with which he was charged, consisted of three unusually solemn gentlemen whose views were such that the view of each differed gloriously from any of the views of the other two.

Three different scientific schools and psychiatric views were represented there.

If in the case of Švejk complete agreement had been reached between opposing scientific camps, it can be explained purely and simply by the stunning impression he produced upon them when he entered the room where his mental state was to be examined and, observing a picture of the Austrian monarch hanging on the wall, cried out:

'Long live our Emperor, Franz Joseph I, gentlemen.'

The case was clear as daylight. Švejk's spontaneous declaration disposed of a whole range of questions, and there only remained a few very important questions which were needed so that from Švejk's answers the initial opinion of him could be confirmed according to the system of the psychiatrist Dr Kallerson, Dr Heveroch and the Englishman, Weiking.

'Is radium heavier than lead?'

'Please sir, I haven't weighed it,' answered Švejk, with his sweet smile.

'Do you believe in the end of the world?'

'I'd have to see that end first,' Švejk answered nonchalantly. 'But certainly I shan't see it tomorrow '

'Would you know how to calculate the diameter of the globe?'

'No, I'm afraid I wouldn't,' answered Švejk, 'but I'd like to ask you a riddle myself, gentlemen. Take a three-storied house, with eight windows on each floor. On the roof there are two dormer windows and two chimneys. On every floor there are two tenants. And now, tell me, gentlemen, in which year the house-porter's grandmother died?'

The medical experts exchanged knowing looks, but nevertheless one of them asked this further question:

'You don't know the maximum depth of the Pacific Ocean?'

'No, please sir, I don't,' was the answer, 'but I think that it must be definitely deeper than the Vltava below the rock of Vyšehrad.'

The chairman of the commission asked briefly: 'Is that enough?', but nonetheless another member requested the following question:

'How much is 12,897 times 13,863?'

'729,' answered Švejk, without batting an eyelid.

'I think that will do,' said the chairman of the commission. 'You can take the accused back where he came from.'

'Thank you, gentlemen,' replied Švejk deferentially. 'For me it will do too.'

After his departure the three agreed that Švejk was a patent imbecile and idiot according to all natural laws invented by the luminaries of pyschiatry.

The report which was passed to the examining magistrate contained inter alia the following:

The undersigned medical experts certify the complete mental feebleness and congenital idiocy of Josef Švejk, who appeared before the aforesaid

(above and following page) *Josef Lada's original illustrations of Good Soldier Švejk*

commission and expressed himself in terms such as: 'Long live our Emperor Franz Joseph I', which utterance is sufficient to illuminate the state of mind of Josef Švejk as that of a patent imbecile.

The undersigned commission accordingly recommends:

1. That the investigation of Josef Švejk be quashed.
2. That Josef Švejk be sent to a psychiatrical clinic for observation to establish how far his mental state is a danger to his surroundings.

While this report was being compiled Švejk was telling his fellow prisoners: 'They didn't care a hoot about Ferdinand, but talked to me about even stupider nonsense. Finally we agreed that what we talked about was quite enough for us and we parted.'

'I don't believe anyone,' observed the short man with a stoop on whose meadow a skeleton happened to have been dug up. 'They're all of them a gang of crooks.'

'There have to be crooks in this world too,' said Švejk, lying down on his straw mattress. 'If everyone were honest with each other, they'd soon start punching each other's noses.'

On duty in the barracks for the second day was Lieutenant Lukáš. All unsuspecting he sat at his desk in the office, when they suddenly brought Švejk to him with the papers.

'Humbly report, sir, I'm here again,' Švejk said, saluting and putting on a solemn expression.

This whole scene was witnessed by Company Sergeant-Major Koťátko, who later related that when Švejk announced himself Lieutenant Lukáš jumped up, put his hands to his head and fell backward on top of Koťátko, and that when they revived him Švejk, who had been saluting all this time, repeated: 'Humbly report, sir, I'm here again!' Then Lieutenant Lukáš, white as a sheet, took with trembling hands the papers which concerned Švejk, signed them, asked everybody to go out, told the gendarme that everything was all right and locked himself into the office together with Švejk.

And so ended Švejk's Budějovice anabasis. It is certain that if Švejk had been granted liberty of movement he would have got to Budňjovice on his own. However much the authorities may boast that it was they who brought Švejk to his place of duty, this is nothing but a mistake. WithŠvejk's energy and irresistible desire to fight, the authorities' action was like throwing a spanner in the works.

Jaroslav Hašek, The Good Soldier Švejk (and his Fortunes in the World War)*, translated by Cecil Parrott with original illustrations by Josef Lada*

From our hero's name comes the term 'Švejkism', often used to characterize the passive resistance of the Czechs during World War II. This classic novel describes the 'little man' fighting officialdom and bureaucracy with the only weapon available to him—passive resistance, subterfuge, native wit and dumb insolence.

Its virile satire and poignancy about the ugliness of war and the utter futility of anything connected with it, inflamed and inspired a nation.

the administration merger with Staré město, a court and a prison were lodged here.

The **Church of St Ignatius** (Kostel sv Ignáce) was where the Jesuits built their second college in 1659. The sculptural work on the façade is the creation of Soldatti and the interior of the church is richly decorated with imitation marble work and statues of Jesuit saints. Since the dissolution of the college in 1770, the complex has served as a hospital.

The present day pharmacy at **Faustus House** (Faustův dům) belies the history behind the building. In the 14th century it was the home of the princess of Opava. After its Renaissance reconstruction, it became famous as the spot where the English adventurer and alchemist Edward Kelly conducted his experiments to produce artificial gold for Emperor Rudolf. In the 18th century the illustrious Ferdinand Mladota performed his brand of scientific magic here. Then, in the 19th century, the house adopted its current name, aided no doubt by neighbourhood gossip, after a student tenant vanished, thought by some to have been taken by the Devil. An oriel and compound corner window are all that remain of the Renaissance period.

Heading west out of the square onto Resslova, you come to the baroque **Church of Sts Cyril and Methodius** (Kostel sv Cyrila a Metoděje), dedicated to the 9th-century monks who brought Christianity to the Slavic people. Take a closer look at the bullet holes in the crypt window, the result of a German assault on six Czechoslovak resistance fighters in 1942. The fighters were responsible for the assassination of the Nazi overlord Reinhard Heydrich, nicknamed the Hangman, and a personal friend of Hitler. To discourage further resistance, Hitler ordered the entire population of Lidice, 450 in all, to be liquidated and the homes and buildings burned.

Less illustrious, but nonetheless a part of Prague, is the **Black Brewery** (Černý pivovar) located on the western side of the square. A rather ugly 1930s building, it is packed daily with locals partaking of the famous dark beer.

A more entertaining spot to drink the same brew (albeit a bit of a tourist trap) is one of Prague's most famous pubs, **U Fleků**, off Resslova on Křemencova. Originally a brewery called Na Křemenci, it is now a popular old pub, restaurant and cabaret. The interior is divided into many rooms, each with its own name. The Velký sál or Great Room is appetizing enough, but what about the Jitrnice, which means liver sausage? The smoke-stained walls are elaborately covered with paintings by Novák. Summer evenings can be whiled away in a tree-shaded beer garden, but be sure to arrive early, as it fills to capacity with merrily singing beer drinkers.

Prague's other famous pub, **At the Chalice Inn** (Hostinec u kalicha), is a popular alehouse serving Pilsner Urquell beer. The interior is decorated to reflect the patronage of its most well-known admirer, the writer Josef Hašek, who created *The Good Soldier Švejk*. 'When the war's over, come and visit me. You'll find me in the Chalice every evening at six,' uttered Švejk. Now the Chalice has become somewhat of a pilgrimage destination.

On Vyšehradská is the **Church of St John Nepomuk on the Rock** (Kostel sv Jana na skalce) and opposite is the eye-catching **Emmaus Monastery** (Kláster na Slovanech), founded by Charles IV for the Croatian Benedictines in 1347. It was his hope that the gesture would help secure his aims for political advancement in south and east Europe.

The work was completed in 1372, in time to be consecrated on Easter Monday of that year. The monastery became an important cultural centre, with studies undertaken in both Old Slavonic and Czech languages. It was here that the famous illuminated Emmaus Bible and part of the Rheims Book of Gospels originated. The original Gothic painted frescoes are still visible in the cloisters but can only be viewed during office hours.

The monastery and church sustained heavy damage in an air raid attack on Valentine's Day 1945, and the two bizarre sail-like buttresses you see today are the imaginative 1965 design of Černý. The monastery has been proclaimed a national cultural monument and currently houses the Institute of the Czechoslovak Academy of Sciences.

The nearby **Prague Botanical Gardens** (Botanická zahrada) are also attributed to Charles IV. Charles' garden started life on the site of the present Main Post Office and led to the creation of a university garden, which was eventually moved to the current site. Though a bit run down now and intended primarily as a place for scientific study, it is conveniently placed and open to the public.

There are several more important churches in the area. **Maria Na Slupi**, on Vyšehradská, with its vault supported by a single pillar, is a rare example of Gothic architecture. The **Church of Our Lady of the Elizabethan Order** is a Dientzenhofer baroque design dating from 1724. Next to the church is the **Chapel of St Tekla** with original 18th-century frescoes by Jan Lukáš. Romantically set on a bluff, the **Church of St John Nepomuk on the Rock** (Kostel sv Jana Nepomuckého na skalce) is yet another Dientzenhofer achievement, built between 1730–1739, eloquently demonstrating his sense of dramatic and theatrical symmetry. On the high altar there is a wooden model of the statue of St John Nepomuk on Charles Bridge. **Charles Church** (Kostel sv Karla Velikého) lies just on the edge of the descent into the Nusle valley. Looming overhead is the imposing Nuselský Bridge, formerly the Clement Gottwald Bridge, which arches across the entire waterless valley.

At the opposite end of the bridge are two of Prague's newer glass structures, the **Forum Hotel**, completed in 1988, and the **Palace of Culture**, opened in 1981. Times have changed since the Palace of Culture's first big event, the 16th Congress of the

Communist Party of Czechoslovakia. Now the main congress hall plays host to conventions, concerts and rallies of all sorts. There is even a casino and a video rental shop in the building.

The Forum Hotel, though lacking in charm, does provide a much needed entertainment centre for visitors and foreign residents. The health club on the top floor is a haven of posh pampering or fitness, whichever you prefer, and the basement bowling alley is crowded nightly with Prague's youthful English speaking set. The first casino to come to Prague also opened here.

Two vastly different museums nestle near the end of the bridge. Walking back down past Charles Church you come to the tiny red palace **Villa Amerika**, housing the Antonín Dvořák museum, a delightful early 18th-century building which was built as a summer palace for the Michna family. His cap and gown are on display as are original music scores, quill pen, eye glasses and souvenirs from his foray into the Western world of Spillville, Iowa.

At the **SNB Police Museum** the silver bust of Lenin is missing from the ominous, gun-lined front hallway, as are several 1940s torture devices. The room dedicated to Felix Dzerzhinsky, the blood-thirsty founder of the Soviet Secret Police, is now denuded of the large holographic portrait whose eyes once followed the visitor around the room. However, it is still worth a visit as the changes are only to make the museum comply with the new political thinking. If the director, Dr Tesař, has his way there will be a new snack bar overlooking the guillotine!

Not far away, at the rocky outcrop of **Vyšehrad**, the trickles of icy cold water from the forest that flow together to become the Vltava reach Prague. According to legend, the rock was destroyed by the marriage of Princess Libuše to her Přemysl farmer. Unfortunately, most of the mystical charm surrounding Vyšehrad and the vision of Princess Libuše have not survived. Her prophesy from this rock about the greatness of Prague, made when women ruled the lands of Bohemia, has somehow been lost in the mists of time. The rock later became an alternative royal residence, when Vratislav II moved there after refusing to live with his hated brother in Prague Castle.

It was not until the last century, when it was inhabited by artists and poets, that Vyšehrad regained any of its former glory. Though there is little of the magnificence of the rest of Prague here, the cobble-stoned streets make for pleasant wandering. The oldest remaining building is the 11th-century **St Martin's Rotunda** (Rotunda sv Martina). Nearby are the remains of the fortified walls constructed in the 14th century by Charles IV. **Vyšehrad Cemetery**, consecrated in the Middle Ages, is now the eternal resting place for most of the country's best loved artists and musicians, including Dvořák and Smetana.

Lesser Town Square from St Nicholas Church with Letná Hill in the background, c. 1940

Malá strana—Lesser Town

The community of markets and tradespeople that gradually expanded on the gently sloping land below Prague Castle (Pražský hrad) came into being as early as the 9th century. The rich west bank of the Vltava between the bluffs of Letná and Petřín hills developed into loosely scattered Romanesque settlements until 1257, when King Přemysl Otakar II declared it Prague's second town and provided it with walls and fortifications.

The location is ideally situated to provide Malá strana, originally called the New Town below Prague Castle, with complete individuality. Separated from the busy Staré město and Nové město by the gently flowing Vltava, it has its own charming island and wide boulevards as well as narrow snaking passageways, small quiet squares and extensive parks.

In its early days, Malá strana was not on equal terms with Staré město, as most of its livelihood was dependent upon the castle. The rights of its citizens were also limited by the jurisdiction of the two monastic orders of St John and St Thomas, which for centuries had administered most of the area independently.

Nonetheless, during the reign of Charles IV the area thrived. A number of Gothic buildings were constructed and the fortifications intensified and widened to encompass more of the outlying communities. This new section of wall is known as the **Hunger Wall**. According to hearsay, Charles IV ordered the building of the section of wall that runs up the southern end of Petřín Hill to provide jobs for the poor and starving. No money was paid for the two years of work, but the labourers were rewarded with life-saving food and clothing.

Unfortunately, an attack by the rebellious Hussites on the royal garrisons of Prague Castle in 1419 devastated the majority of the buildings. Though life gradually returned to normal towards the end of the century, the Great Fire of 1541 destroyed most of what had been rebuilt. This time, however, there was widespread Renaissance building activity and ambitious large scale remodelling of the area.

After the Battle of White Mountain in 1620 ended the Thirty Years' War, many wealthy families loyal to the victorious Hapsburgs moved to the area. Ostentatious palaces, churches and monasteries begin to take root, leading eventually to the style that became famous as Prague baroque. Magnificent summer gardens were created around the homes which, when combined with the existing green expanses of Petřín and Letná hills, became a playground for the European aristocracy. In 1784, Malá strana ceased to exist as a separate entity and became one of united Prague's most desirable districts. Though its status declined when power reverted to Vienna, Malá strana has remained the 'in' place to live.

Lesser Town Square (Malostranské náměstí) at the heart of the district is dominated by the high baroque masterpiece of **St Nicholas Church** (Kostel sv Mikuláše), which divides the square into two parts. The church, whose distinctive basilica façade can be admired from most vantage points in Prague, was designed by Kristof Dientzenhofer in 1704. The choir and dome were later additions by his son, Kilian Ignaz. Anselmo Lurago completed the building in the mid-18th century with the addition of the belfry tower. The ceiling fresco above the main nave, painted by Jan Lukáš Kracker in 1761, portrays scenes from St Nicholas' life. At 1,500 square metres (16,146 square feet), it is one of the largest paintings in Europe. Another magnificent fresco in the 75-metre (246-foot)-high dome, the *Celebration of the Holiest Trinity*, is by Franz Xavier Palko. Standing by the pillars in the nave are wooden stucco statues of St Nicholas by Platzer the Elder. The church is open daily from 09:00 to 16:00 and printed guide sheets are provided.

Adjacent to St Nicholas is the former Jesuit College which took over the land of the Romanesque Rotunda of St Wenceslas. Much renovation and reconstruction occurred, and the final phases were completed in 1691 by Lurago. Opposite the church, enclosing the entire northern end of the square, is the imposing neo-classical **Lichtenstein Palace**. It takes its name from the 'Bloody Governor' Karel of Lichtenstein, notorious for his remorseless persecution of the anti-Hapsburg leaders and his mass executions in Old Town Square.

Just down the square is one of the purest Renaissance houses in Malá strana, the **Golden Lion** (U zlatého lva). Treat yourself and make a reservation at the wine bar here, **U Mecenáše**: the food is excellent and the décor has enchanted diners since the early 17th century. A few steps away is the pub **U Glaubiců**, a great place for beer and cold snacks.

The lower side of the square, where the tram tracks cross, is bordered by **Café Malostranská Kavárna**, a superb coffee and wine spot with a delightful outdoor terrace in summer, and the **Kaiserstein Palace**. The plaque on the façade denotes the latter as the former home of the well-known opera singer Emmy Destinn. Next door is the former town hall of Malá strana. Today it is used as a jazz club, and the great hall hosts some of Prague's more elegant social occasions—little imagination is required to transport oneself back in time to the days of brocade frock coats, powdered wigs, romantic chamber music and masked balls.

Mostecká, leading down to Charles Bridge, is a lively spot filled with strolling tourists, a movie theatre (check the schedule for English-language films), coffee and wine bars, antique shops and an assortment of souvenir shops. The side streets display an endless array of plaques in memory of the various people who have slept or lived in the houses, such as Czar Peter the Great, René Châteaubriand and Ludwig van Beethoven.

House of the Three Fiddles on Nerudova, home to the Edlinger violin makers from 17th–18th century

Next wend your way off Mostecká to **Maltese Square** (Maltézské náměstí) and the former **Nostitz Palace** which dates from the 17th century. A tiny portion is now oc-cupied by the Dutch Embassy. You will also see the beautiful roco-co building occupied by the Japa-nese Embassy, the former **Turba Palace**.

The group of statues in the cen-tre of the square is a Brokoff crea-tion representing St John the Baptist and commemorates the end of the plague epidemic.

In the church of **St Mary be-neath the Chain** (Kostel Panny Marie pod řetězem) you can visit the beautiful baroque interior of the oldest church in Malá strana. The remains of its 12th-century Romanesque basilica can still be seen.

Tucked to one side and slightly behind St Mary's is the **House at the Painters** (Dům u malířů), one of Prague's finest but most expensive restaurants. The building retains its 1531 Renaissance layout, and Gothic fortifications can be seen in the su-perb wine cellars which house some of the restaurant's US$100 plus French wines.

Also located near St Mary's Church is Grand Prior's Square (Velkopřevorské náměstí), where the French Embassy now resides in the **Buquoy Palace**. Opposite is the former **Grand Prior of the Knights of Malta Palace**, still one of the finest in Malá strana, which houses the **Museum of Musical Instruments**. In the Maltese Gardens you can listen to fabulous outdoor concerts during the summer months.

On the edge of the square you will notice a small bridge leading to **Kampa Island**, one of the prettiest corners of Malá strana, across a small branch of the Vltava called Čertovka (Devil's Stream). The name most probably originated from the nickname of an eccentric woman owner of the **House At the Seven Devils** (Dům u sedmi čertů). The island is actually the only part of Prague that one might say benefitted from the Great Fire of 1541, as rubble and debris from the destroyed buildings were pushed onto the banks providing more stability than before. At first only Sova's Mills, vine-yards and gardens covered the island, but by the latter half of the 16th century and the early 17th century construction began on elegant homes in the northern part and lovely gardens to the south.

The name Kampa came from the Latin word *campus*, meaning field, as the area was largely covered in lush parkland. The old ferryman's house, dating from the days when ferries were the fastest means of transport to Staré město, has been preserved in the street U Sovových mlynů. The stairs leading to Charles Bridge were first constructed of wood in 1844. If you follow them down to **Kampa Square** (Na Kampě) you will discover the best place in Prague to buy fabulous Czech pottery and ceramics, a tradition that began in the 16th century. There are also outdoor markets here at weekends and the occasional festival well worth visiting.

Passing under Charles Bridge you can walk up beside one of Prague's prettiest small hotels, **House at the Three Ostriches** (Dům u tří pštrosů), erected in 1585 in

front of the larger tower at the head of Charles Bridge. In 1597 the building became the property of Jan Fux, a merchant of ostrich feathers which were a fashion novelty at the time. This is also where the Armenian Deodat Damajan founded Prague's first coffee house in 1714 (see Coffee Houses page 144). Between 1972 and 1976, the magnificent coloured façade was repaired and the building converted into a hotel. The superb ground floor restaurant dates from the 17th century and is also known to be one of the favourite eateries of Václav Havel.

Many of the former palaces in the area now house embassies, museums and government ministries. Just down Tomášská, off Lesser Town Square (Malostranské náměstí), is the grandest and most opulent of all the baroque palaces in Malá strana, **Waldstein Palace** (Valdštejnský palác). Seeing the dreary palace walls from the street gives no impression of

Spire of Strahov Monastery

the staggering beauty inside. Designed and built exclusively by Italians between 1624 and 1630, the palace was intended to outshine the castle complex. In many ways it succeeds. The owner was an enormously wealthy imperial generalissimo, Albrecht von Waldstein, who was dubbed Duke of Friedland and allowed to purchase much confiscated property belonging to Czech nobility after the Battle of White Mountain. His palace consisted of five interconnecting courtyards and a marvellous garden built over the razed land where 25 houses once stood. Even the city gate was not spared in Waldstein's grandiose plans.

The splendid Italianate garden has a wide, sweeping avenue lined with replicas of mythological bronze statues by Adrien de Vreis, court sculptor to Emperor Rudolf II. The originals were stolen as booty during the Thirty Years' War and taken to reside in the grounds of Drottningholm Palace near Stockholm, where they remain today. There are also fountains and beautiful ponds. According to locals, the first steam-powered boat engine was tested in the large round pond. Social events and gallery exhibitions now take place in the former riding school nearby.

At the other end of the garden is the triple arched loggia **Sala Terrena**, decorated with stunning frescoes. To one side is an artificial grotto with a wall of stalactites and stalagmites ending in an aviary full of strutting peacocks.

Waldstein was not destined to enjoy his palace for long, however. He was caught double-dealing with the enemy and Ferdinand II, who began to doubt his loyalty, had him murdered in 1634.

During the week the garden is remarkably free of people: at the weekend there are open-air concerts in the loggia. The gardens are open from May to September, Tuesday to Sunday 10:00–18:00. The entrance is on Letenská.

After visiting the gardens, head straight up Letenská to the **Monastery of St Thomas** (Klášter sv Tomáše), founded in 1285 by King Wenceslas II. The main part of the monastery serves as a home for senior citizens. In the basement is the restaurant U Tomáše. The brewery, founded as early as 1358, was moved to the basement here in 1763 and has been a popular alehouse ever since. Open all year round, the main restaurant is in the original brewery and caters to large tour groups so it can be crowded and a bit noisy. They also have a small selection of Bohemian crystal for sale. In summer there is an outdoor garden with a delicious barbecue.

Walking back up Tomášská, you will pass one of the finest examples of Prague's house signs, the **Golden Stag** (U zlatého jelena), an ornate depiction of St Hubert and a stag by Maximilian Brokoff. Wander through the streets in this area and you will discover many fine palaces and squares once owned by powerful Bohemian families such as **Lobkovic, Kolowrat** and **Černín**. Along **Valdštejnská** you pass the terraced grounds of the Polish Embassy, which are not open to the public, and four other fabulous gardens that can be visited.

St Nicholas Church, Malá strana, c. 1940

Several of the foreign embassies are housed in former palaces lining the streets of Vlašská and Nerudova and the beautiful Maltese and Grand Priory squares. The American Embassy in the **Schönborn Palace** at Tržiště No 15 nestles amongst a broad expanse of park grounds in the shadow of Petřín Hill. The carved house gate is preserved from the original Renaissance building. Another street worth prowling is Sněmovní ulička where tiny cul-de-sacs provide an assortment of house signs, a few good local pubs and some charming gardens. Continue in the direction of Thunovská ulička and you will reach the **New Castle Steps** leading up to the castle. Note these are actually much older than the old castle steps.

Parallel to the New Castle Steps is **Nerudova**, lined with superb house signs. One of Prague's best watering holes is located in the Renaissance **House at the Cat** (Dům u kocoura) at No 2. The **Three Fiddles** (U tří housliček) is at No 12, where the well-known Edlinger family of violin-makers lived. The Italian Embassy, decorated with two enormous eagles and the statues of Jupiter and Juno is at No 20, the former **Thun-Hohenstein Palace**. The Romanian Embassy is located in the **Morzin Palace**, where two giant heraldic Moors support the balcony.

The most famous house in the street is the **House of the Two Suns** (Dům u dvou slunců), a fine example of early baroque with splendid gables and a Renaissance portal. This was the home of writer Jan Neruda (1834–1891), in whose honour a large memorial tablet was constructed on the façade in 1895. The street is now filled with galleries, wine bars and antique shops, plus a tiny pharmacological museum in the former pharmacy at **The Golden Lion.**

The **Monastery of the Theatines** is beside the New Castle Steps. At the top of Nerudova you can either follow the road up into Ke Hradu to gain a fabulous view of sgraffito-covered **Schwarzenberg Palace**, or take the steps up to the western end of Castle Square (Hradčanské náměstí). If you go straight on, leave Malá strana in the direction of **Strahov Monastery** (Strahovský klášter).

At the top of Nerudova you will see the magnificent rococo **Bretfeld Palace**, re-built in 1765 on the site of a baroque burgher's house to a Wirch design. The relief of St Nicholas on the façade is the work of Ignaz Franz Platzer. In 1787 both the composer Wolfgang Amadeus Mozart and the notorious Giovanni Casanova stayed here and certainly attended some of the elaborate balls held in the grand ballroom.

As you continue to the last house pay special attention to the house signs. At No 220, the **House at the Golden Horseshoe**, there is a real horseshoe on the foot of a horse. Houses Nos 235 and 236, which were connected in 1968, display the sculptured reliefs of a red lion with a golden cup in his paws and a lobster adorned with a stucco floral design.

Now follow the winding steps and passage into Šporkova ulička, along the tree lined ridge of the Petřín Valley into Vlašská ulička, just opposite **Lobkovic Palace**,

House sign, Malá strana

home of the German Embassy, which gained fame as the temporary camping ground for thousands of East Germans in 1989. **Lobkovická Vinárna**, a wine bar, is located at No 17 in a house that was built for a favourite mistress.

To visit **Petřín Hill** with its beautiful parks and wonderful follies now follow Vlašská ulička to the right, or if you prefer to try the **funicular**, go in the opposite direction and walk up the steps to the ticket office. The original funicular was run by a system built in 1891 that used a water tank at the top, which, by emptying at the bottom, powered the cars going up solely by the weight of the cars going down. You can see pictures and a working demonstration at the top landing. One stop is made halfway up the hill at the restaurant **Nebozízek**, which offers fine dining and good views.

The park, **St Laurence's Hill**, was created by the linking of several gardens and a former vineyard. A path at the top of the hill leads all the way through the park to **Strahov Monastery**. You can also visit the Ethnographic Museum set up in **Villa Kinsky.**

The best part of the park, however, is a stroll through the remains of the Jubilee Exhibition of 1891. The most obvious site is the iron **Observation Tower** built as a copy of the Eiffel Tower in Paris. There is also a fun house mirror maze and a diorama depicting *The Battle of Prague Students Against the Swedes on Charles Bridge* in 1648.

The attractive gardens of **Ledebour, Palffy, Černín** and **Furstenberg palaces** extend over the southern slope below Prague Castle. Dating from the Middle Ages, when numerous vineyards covered the area, the gardens were laid out as integral parts of the elaborate noble palaces. In the 18th century the magnificent *sala terrena* was built and decorated with murals depicting the explosion of Vesuvius, the ruins of Pompeii and mythological scenes. There are other fine frescoes scattered throughout the gardens, as well as terraces, enchanting fountains and pools, balustrades and loggias. In summer the gardens are a riot of colour.

Bohemian tinkers, from a drawing by Walter Crane

Czech Crystal and Glassware

The tradition of fine glass-making in Bohemia dates all the way back to the days of the Celts. In the 8th and 10th centuries the craft developed, concentrated in the area known as the Great Moravian Empire. By the 19th century, **Moser Crystal**, the glass of kings, was renowned for its pure, flawless character and elegant cuts.

In 1857, Ludvik Moser, a former student of the well-known engraver A H Mattoni, founded a decorating workshop with a representative shop at Karlovy Vary. At that time, Karlovy Vary was not only an important spa, but also a cultural and social centre. The favourable atmosphere which evolved in the town attracted artists, who were commissioned by eminent spa guests from all over the world to engrave their portraits. Later, in 1893, Moser founded his own glassworks at nearby Dvory, where a modern glassworks, known as the Karlovarské Sklo (Moser National Corporation), still produces hand-blown glass in the traditional manner.

Moser products quickly gained an excellent international reputation thanks to their first-class quality, and in the early 20th century Bohemian glass blowers were chosen to create the designs of Vienna's famous Wiener Werkstätte. The glassworks continued to concentrate on the manufacture of art and de luxe glass and were appointed court supplier both to the imperial court in Vienna and to the English king. The European royal courts remain some of Moser's greatest patrons.

The first Moser engravings on glass depicted figural scenes, hunting motifs and spa themes. Engraved ornaments, initials and emblems were all of the same high quality seen today. After 1900, characteristic series of Moser tableware were gradually developed, bringing the glassworks new renown. Some of these sets are still in production and combine simple shapes of very refined proportions to which various types of cuts are applied. An etched matt gilded ornamental border is used on many of their products. Variants of this decoration adorn not only table glass, but also vases, bowls and ashtrays of both transparent and coloured glass.

Souvenir seekers, however, should note the difference between ordinary glass and crystal. Crystal is at least 24 per cent lead and reflects more light than glass. Crystal is also easier to engrave, producing a flat decoration, or cut, which gives a three-dimensional effect. The lead content of each piece is generally designated by a sticker. Crystal costs up to twice as much as its glass equivalent. Of course, the intricacy of engraving or cutting can also raise the price considerably, as can handblowing over machine production.

In spite of privatization, Czech glass and crystal are still good buys in the Czech Republic. Prices for an equivalent piece back home can be at least 50 per cent higher. Be sure to check on duty charges before you make a big purchase, however. At one time there was a 300 per cent duty on crystal chandeliers. Another good rule to remember is to buy something you like when you see it. Stocks change daily and supplies run very low in peak tourist times. Beware of the quality at some of the street vendors.

In Prague, the most well-known and luxurious shop is the mahogany-panelled 19th-century Moser building on Na příkopě. This is the main outlet for the company, but the factory and museum in Karlovy Vary are still interesting to visit. Though Moser does not make lead crystal, all its products are hand-blown. It specializes in coloured vases, boxes and bowls, which are usually thick pieces of geometric design, and clear stemware with simple lines.

Between the two World Wars Moser conducted fascinating experiments with coloured glass. Rare earths were used to give the glass refined colour shades. In the 1930s, simple cut coloured glass became a successful, characteristic product of the Moser Glassworks. The wide range of unusual hues is still applied in the production of various types of de luxe glass known collectively under the name of *Fantazie*. This designation comprises vases, jardinières and bowls, decorated either with facet or irregular plastic cut. Due to their typical colours and cut, these products resemble a synthetic semi-precious stone rather than ordinary glass.

Moser customers can pay for their purchases with major credit cards or hard currencies, as well as Czech crowns. Purchases can be shipped abroad, though that is not advisable because of the lengthy delay, averaging about eight months to America.

If you prefer leaded crystal, **Bohemia Glassworks**, which has factories scattered throughout the northern region, offers chunky cut pieces of very high quality. Visitors can find a good selection of glass and crystal brands, including Moser, at Bohemia's Prague shop. Bohemia's wide choice of crystal products occasionally includes platters and decanters, and crystal chandeliers are available in both traditional and modern designs. This is a good place to acquire one of the country's signature designs, the intricately cut lace pattern, with panels that divide the object into spheres containing star bursts and sun motifs. Though they do not offer shipping facilities, they do accept credit cards as well as Czech crowns.

The glassworks at Harrachov, home of **Crystalex**, ranks amongst the oldest in Europe. According to documents found it was established as long ago as 1712, though it was not, by far, the earliest in the region. In the 18th and 19th centuries the best engravings were executed on Harrachov crystal and it was from this region that the leading glass engravers obtained their raw material. The company also won the top award at the World Exhibition in London in 1851.

Crystalex specializes in contemporary artistic creations, both machine-made and hand-blown. The company is now the country's largest manufacturer of all types of glassware including household glass, art glass and crystal and has attained outstanding results, particularly in the production of crystal.

Bohemian Crystal

The Rebelliousness of Old Age

Historical events usually imitate one another without much talent, but in Czechoslovakia, as I see it, history staged an unprecedented experiment. Instead of the standard pattern of one group of people (a class, a nation) rising up against another, all the people (an entire generation) revolted against their own youth.

Their goal was to recapture and tame the deed they had created, and they almost succeeded. All through the 1960s they gained in influence, and by the beginning of 1968 their influence was virtually complete. This is the period commonly referred to as the Prague Spring: the men guarding the idyll had to go around removing microphones from private dwellings, the borders were opened, and notes began abandoning the score of Bach's grand fugue and singing their own lines. The spirit was unbelievable. A real carnival!

Russia, composer of the master fugue for the globe, could not tolerate the thought of notes taking off on their own. On August 21, 1968, it sent an army of half a million men into Bohemia. Shortly thereafter, about a hundred and twenty thousand Czechs left their country, and of those who remained about five hundred thousand had to leave their jobs for manual labor in the country, at the conveyor belt of an out-of-the-way factory, behind the steering wheel of a truck—in other words, for places and jobs where no one would ever hear their voices.

And just to be sure not even the shadow of an unpleasant memory could come to disturb the newly revived idyll, both the Prague Spring and the Russian tanks, that stain on the nation's fair history, had to be nullified. As a result, no one in Czechoslovakia commemorates the 21st of August, and the names of the people who rose up against their own youth are carefully erased from the nation's memory, like a mistake from a homework assignment.

Mirek's was one of the names thus erased. The Mirek currently climbing *the stairs to Zdena's door is really only a white stain, a fragment of barely delineated void making its way up a spiral staircase.*

Milan Kundera, The Book of Laughter and Forgetting, *1980*

A native Czech, Milan Kundera has been living and working in France since 1975. After the publication of The Book Of Laughter And Forgetting, *the Czech Government revoked his citizenship. He has won several prizes for literature, including the* Los Angeles Times Prize *for* The Unbearable Lightness Of Being.

Alexander Dubček, President of Czechoslovakia in 1968

Hradčany

Throughout the history of Prague people have lived around the castle. The original community of castle serfs broadened during the construction of the Hunger Wall in 1360–1362. After the destruction during the Hussite Wars, the area did not begin to thrive again until the 15th century. The Great Fire of 1541 destroyed many buildings and gave new impetus for wealthy families to erect majestic Renaissance homes near the castle. Burghers' houses, the palaces of nobility and church dignitaries as well as monasteries soon filled the area.

In 1598, Hradčany was raised to the status of a royal town and remained as such until 1784 when it became one of the districts of a united Prague. Hradčany is still much as it was in the 17th and 18th centuries when the baroque brick fortification walls were constructed.

Hradčany Square (Hradčanské náměstí) emerged after the Great Fire, the creation of noble families wishing to enhance their own status and impress the neighbouring royals. Their perch above the city offers a stunning view of Prague and Petřín Hill.

The first of the grand palaces to be built was **Schwarzenberg Palace** (Schwarzenberský palác) at the top of Nerudova. The construction was undertaken by the Lobkovic family and took from 1545 until 1563. The façade, with its gables and projecting lunette cornice, is covered in diamond sgraffito in Italian Renaissance style while the interior ceilings are of hand-painted canvas stretched over wooden frames. Today the palace houses the Museum of Military History and a collection of early arms and uniforms.

Directly across the square is the **Palace of the Archbishop of Prague** (Arcibiskupský palác). Originally constructed in 1562 in Renaissance style, it underwent a transformation between 1675 and 1684 to emerge as early baroque. The richly decorated rococo façade of today was added in 1764–1765 and bears the archbishop's coat-of-arms and sculptures by Ignaz Franz Platzer. The interior, filled with period furniture, fine wood cuts and collections of glass and china, is only open once a year on Maundy Thursday.

Tucked down a narrow alley to the left and completely obscured by the Archbishop's Palace is the baroque **Sternberg Palace** (Šternberský palác). This is now the main building of the **National Gallery** and houses a superb collection of European art including works by Breughel, Dürer, Rubens, Edvard Munch and the French Impressionists. Enter through the arch to the far left of the front of the Archbishop's Palace.

Antique shop in Hradčany

At the western end of the square is the early baroque **Toscani Palace** which dates from 1690 and has statues of the Gods of Antiquity decorating the attic ledge. Also on the western side is **Martinic Palace**, built in 1700 by the imperial ambassador to Rome. Some of the original sgraffito decorations, representing Bible scenes and dating back to the 16th century, have been discovered beneath the façade.

The south side of the square leads to the castle ramp and the Café Kajetánka. In the middle of the square stands a plague column engraved with a statue of the Virgin Mary and figures of the eight patrons of the Bohemian provinces.

After a cool refreshment at **U labutí** (The Swan), follow the cobblestone road away from the square in the direction of Strahov Monastery and listen as you go to the delightful sound of bells pealing around the palaces. This tradition goes back to the days of the plague when a distressed mother paid for the church bells to be rung whenever one of her children died. When the plague also claimed the life of the woman, the area fell silent until, mysteriously, all the bells of the Loreta rang out in the tune of a famous hymn, and have continued to do so ever since.

As you enter **Loreta Square** (Loretánské náměstí) in the area called **Nový Svět** (New World) you will notice two contrasting sights. On the left is the massive **Černín Palace** built in Italian Palladium style. Home of the imperial ambassador to Venice during the 17th century, it is now the seat of the Ministry of Foreign Affairs.

Across the road in a tree-shrouded pastoral idyll stands the Loreta, encircling the secretive and treasured **Santa Casa Shrine**. The shrine is modelled on the Lauretanian House in Italy, which according to legend was the house of the Virgin Mary, transferred there from the Holy Land. Over the centuries, the shrine became the centre of Catholicism and a place of pilgrimage for visiting nobility, who made valuable votive offerings. Many of these items can be viewed upstairs in the Loreta Treasury, including the incredible and renowned **Diamond Monstrance**. The oldest work of art is a 1510 Gothic chalice decorated with enamelled miniatures.

In the vaulted arcades opposite Černín Palace are antique shops and art galleries. For a taste of the local 12° dark beer, drop in to **U cerného vola** (The Little Black Ox), which used to be a good place to mingle with the locals until the soaring beer prices drove them away. The best time to wander by the winebar **U zlaté hrušky** (At the Golden Pear) is in the early evening. In the spring, umbrella-shaded tables appear on the terrace in front of the 18th-century stucco façade. Afterwards, stroll through the narrow winding alleys past tiny cottages clinging to the steep edges. Once considered the poor sector below the castle, the area is now home to many artists, writers and intellectuals.

Now head back towards Pohořelec which runs west from the far end of the square. As you walk towards **Strahov Monastery** be careful not to miss the remains of the Kurz Summer Palace tucked in the courtyard of the school at the corner of

Theological Hall, Strahov Monastery library, c. 1940

Parléřova. This was where the Danish astronomer Tycho Brahe lived from 1559 until he died in 1601. The group of statues represents Brahe and his German counterpart Johann Kepler, who stayed with him here to carry out astronomical observations.

STRAHOV MONASTERY

The lush green northern slope of Petřín Hill is dominated by the distinctive twin spired silhouette of the **Strahov Monastery** (Strahovský klášter). It was founded in 1140 by Prince Vladislav II, and is the oldest Premonstratensian monastery in Bohemia. Originally the monastery had its own fortifications as, until the construction of the Hunger Wall in the early 14th century, it lay outside the fortifications of Hradčany. Despite its turbulent history and bouts of reconstruction, the monks and canons of Strahov still managed to amass one of the most extensive and most valuable libraries in the country.

The monastery remained in active religious pursuit for over eight hundred years until 1952, when the Czech State dissolved all religious orders in Czechoslovakia. Strahov Monastery was declared the **Museum of National Literature**, a purpose it still serves. The 130,000 volumes possessed by the library in 1950 have increased to an impressive 900,000 tomes, in addition to 5,000 illuminated manuscripts. One of the most famous, the library's oldest manuscript, is the 9th-century Strahov Gospels.

The manuscripts are housed in the original early baroque library called the **Theological Hall**, built by Giovanni Domenico Orsi during the 1670s. In the centre of the hall are 17th-century geographical and astronomical globes. The magnificent ceiling frescoes painted by Siard Nosecký, a member of the monastery, and the stucco cartouches eulogize learning and books.

One hundred years after its foundation, the Old Library was supplemented by the **Philosophical Hall**, built by Giovanni Palliardi with ceiling frescoes by Frantisek A Maulpertsch. The work was carried out in Viennese rococo style and depicts the theme of *The Struggle of Mankind to Know Real Wisdom*. The ornamental vases and decorative objects are the work of Ignaz Franz Platzer. The most valuable fittings are the walnut cabinets and bookshelves designed by Lachhover and transferred from the Moravian monastery of Louka. The marble bust of the Emperor Franz I was sculpted by Lederer.

The Late Renaissance **Church of St Roch** (Kostel sv Rocha) was the original Strahov parish church. It was built by the Emperor Rudolf II between 1603 and 1612, during the time of Abbot Jan Lohelius, as an expression of gratitude when the plague was averted. During the 17th and 18th centuries the building underwent extensive alteration and was richly decorated in striking Gothic style. The Musaion exhibition hall is now housed here.

The monastery is surrounded by large gardens laid out in park style stretching through the valley of the Petřín Hills over to the edge of Malá strana. This beautiful view of Prague, accessible to the public from Úvoz, attracts large numbers of strollers along its observation path.

PRAGUE CASTLE

There was a time at the beginning of 1990 when Prague Castle was ablaze with a zany new freedom. The hordes of tourists had not yet reached full impact and a newly elected, handsome young President Václav Havel could be seen about the grounds wearing Western jeans and an enormous smile. He worked with everyone, including the equally new young guard of honour, as they practised their recently choreographed movements. Occasionally he would walk alongside one of the boys and demonstrate how to move his arms or legs in pseudo soldier-like manner. Often he would point to a uniform and gesture about the design of an epaulette or the length of the trousers. But with the passing of time, routines formed and the job of president became more tedious. Now he can only be seen surrounded by an entourage of body guards and minders and rarely in his favourite jeans. The castle, however, as presidential seat and political and cultural centre of the nation is still ablaze and remains one of Prague's favourite monuments both for local residents and visitors. Its history, steeped in legend, is reflected in the millennium-long period of its construction.

Prague Castle and St Vitus' Cathedral from the Smetana Museum

Prague Castle

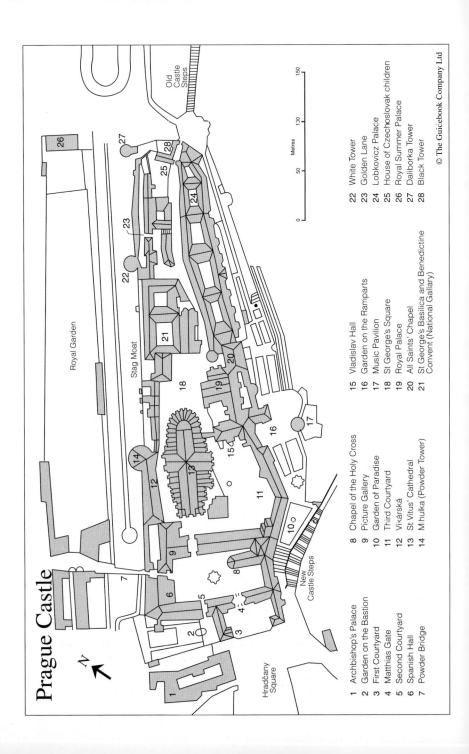

Hradčany Square

Royal Garden

Old Castle Steps

Stag Moat

New Castle Steps

© The Guidebook Company Ltd

Metres
0   50   100   150

1 Archbishop's Palace
2 Garden on the Bastion
3 First Courtyard
4 Matthias Gate
5 Second Courtyard
6 Spanish Hall
7 Powder Bridge

8 Chapel of the Holy Cross
9 Picture Gallery
10 Garden of Paradise
11 Third Courtyard
12 Vikárská
13 St Vitus' Cathedral
14 Mihulka (Powder Tower)

15 Vladislav Hall
16 Garden on the Ramparts
17 Music Pavilion
18 St George's Square
19 Royal Palace
20 All Saints' Chapel
21 St George's Basilica and Benedictine
     Convent (National Gallery)

22 White Tower
23 Golden Lane
24 Lobkovicz Palace
25 House of Czechoslovak children
26 Royal Summer Palace
27 Daliborka Tower
28 Black Tower

From the beginning, the castle has been surrounded by a sense of romance. According to the oldest Czech chronicle written by Cosmas, the 12th-century dean of the Chapter of St Vitus, it is where Princess Libuše related her vision of a big city whose glory would touch the stars to her consort, Prince Přemysl. Not only did this vision lead to the founding of a dynasty, but it has served as a source of inspiration for hundreds of years of Bohemian art and literature. Legend apart, the castle is most definitely the oldest continually inhabited area of Prague.

The castle was founded in the late 9th century on a headland above the Vltava Valley, long since the crossroads of important trans-European trade routes, and became the natural seat of the dynasty. The first wooden fort was constructed by Prince Bořivoj on a pagan worship site which, according to legend, provoked a pagan uprising in the country and led to his temporary exile. Shortly afterwards the first church was built and consecrated to Our Lady. At the beginning of the 10th century, Vratislav I founded St George's Church, the second of Prague Castle's churches, close to the Prince's Palace, and between the years 926 and 930 Prince Václav built the Church of St Vitus, a rotunda with four apses. In 973 the bishopric of Prague was founded.

In the 11th century, under the rule of Prince Břatislav I, the earthen ramparts were replaced with stone fortifications, and the construction begun by Prince Soběslav a 100 years earlier entered a period of haphazard enlargement and constant modification until the rule of Empress Maria Theresa (1740–1780). The empress commissioned the Viennese court architect Nicolo Pacassi to undertake the vast project of unifying the façades of the various buildings to transform the castle into the single magnificent palace we see today. Only one aspect of Prague Castle remained constant for more than 1,000 years: its planned mission. From the end of the 9th century until 1918, the castle was the official residence and place of coronation of Czech sovereigns and, since 1918, it has been the presidential seat of the Czech and Slovak Republic—and latterly of the Czech Republic. It can be described as the tru heart of the nation.

Elevated to the status of a royal seat and centre of the vast Holy Roman Empire, the castle experienced its period of greatest wealth during the reign of Charles IV (1346–1378). The famous architect Matthias of Arras was called in to design the Romanesque basilica of the Gothic **St Vitus' Cathedral** for the newly founded archbishopric in 1344. Other well-known designers, including Petr Parléř, were consulted up until the Hussite Wars, which brought to a close the first great period in the castle's history. During the Hussite Wars the castle area suffered appreciable damage and, though still used for coronations, the royal family did not take up residency again until the reign of Rudolf II (1576–1611).

The whimsical Emperor Rudolf, who was more interested in the arts, astrology and alchemy than ruling, surrounded himself with widely diverse art collections and curiosities for which he built new halls. Artists and craftsmen from all over Europe spent time at the castle during his reign and each contributed to its changing appearance and growing artistic treasures. Rudolf's successor, Matthias, instigated the construction of the baroque **Matthias Gate**.

After suppression of the anti-Hapsburg insurrection and the subsequent removal of all important institutions and government departments to Vienna, the castle ceased to be a royal residence. It fell from glory, rating as a mere weekend retreat from Vienna.

Architectural development stagnated during the Thirty Years' War (1618–1648), during which time Prague suffered further insult when the Swedes appropriated valuable collections during their occupation of the castle.

After the wave of construction carried out under Empress Maria Theresa in the 18th century, it was not until the first half of the 19th century that the castle experienced a brief period of revival. The coronation of Emperor Ferdinand V (1835–1848) marked the last coronation in Prague, as his successor, Joseph I, did not have himself crowned King of Bohemia, although preparations were made at the castle for the event.

■ FIRST AND SECOND COURTYARDS

The first courtyard (první nádvoří) of the castle complex is the newest, dating from Maria Theresa's reconstructions between 1763–1771. The massive ornamental gate and grille are topped by replicas of the imposing statues of the *Battling Titans* by Ignaz Platzer the Elder. The young guards of honour posted on either side are changed every hour on the hour and, unlike the stone-faced guards at Buckingham Palace, are known to smile on occasion.

Just opposite the main gateway stands the baroque **Matthias Gate**, created by Emperor Matthias in 1614 as a separate triumphal arch. The gate, now set into a new section that is also part of Maria Theresa's reconstructions, houses various presidential reception rooms and serves as the entrance to the second courtyard (druhé nádvoří). To the left of the first courtyard lies the **Garden on the Bastion** (Zahrada na baště), which is accessible from Hradčanské náměstí (Castle Square). On the northern side of the garden is the entrance to the **Spanish Hall** (Španělský sál) and the **Rudolf Gallery** (Rudofova galerie). The Spanish Hall was prepared for the coronation of Joseph I, who refused the ceremony, and was not used until it was refitted with mirrors in 1836 for the coronation of Ferdinand V.

The **Picture Gallery** (Obrazárna Pražského hradu) is located in the second courtyard in the ground floor halls which once formed elaborate stables. During renovation, the remains of the original Church of Our Lady, founded in the 9th century by

Battling Giants, the main gate of Prague Castle

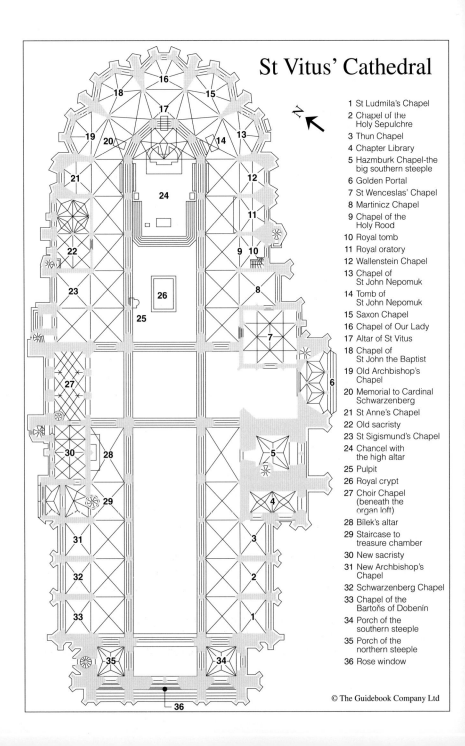

St Vitus' Cathedral

1 St Ludmila's Chapel
2 Chapel of the
  Holy Sepulchre
3 Thun Chapel
4 Chapter Library
5 Hazmburk Chapel-the
  big southern steeple
6 Golden Portal
7 St Wenceslas' Chapel
8 Martinicz Chapel
9 Chapel of the
  Holy Rood
10 Royal tomb
11 Royal oratory
12 Wallenstein Chapel
13 Chapel of
   St John Nepomuk
14 Tomb of
   St John Nepomuk
15 Saxon Chapel
16 Chapel of Our Lady
17 Altar of St Vitus
18 Chapel of
   St John the Baptist
19 Old Archbishop's
   Chapel
20 Memorial to Cardinal
   Schwarzenberg
21 St Anne's Chapel
22 Old sacristy
23 St Sigismund's Chapel
24 Chancel with
   the high altar
25 Pulpit
26 Royal crypt
27 Choir Chapel
   (beneath the
   organ loft)
28 Bílek's altar
29 Staircase to
   treasure chamber
30 New sacristy
31 New Archbishop's
   Chapel
32 Schwarzenberg Chapel
33 Chapel of the
   Bartoňs of Dobenín
34 Porch of the
   southern steeple
35 Porch of the
   northern steeple
36 Rose window

Prince Bořivoj, were discovered. Those parts of the eccentric Emperor Rudolf II's collections not looted or auctioned off are housed here. The gallery display includes some valuable works by Titian, Rubens, Tintoretto and Veronese, as well as important sculptural works by Braun and Czech baroque pieces by Jan Kupecký and Petr Brandle.

The eastern side of this second courtyard contains the **White Tower** and the remains of the Romanesque fortifications of Soběslav I. You will find a post office situated on the ground floor of the tower with reception rooms and archives above.

Be sure to visit the **Chapel of the Holy Cross** (Kaple u sv kříže) in the southeast corner. This is where the most valuable pieces of the cathedral treasure are kept, including the helmet and chainmail shirt of St Wenceslas (9th and 10th century), the 10th-century sword of St Stephen and a richly ornamented gold Gothic coronation cross from the 14th century. A baroque fountain by stonemason Francesco de Torre plays in the centre of the courtyard. Near the fountain is a well covered with an artistically decorated iron grille. The fountain with the lion is a more recent work (1965–1967) by the sculptor Makovský and architect Fragner.

■ THE THIRD COURTYARD

The **third courtyard** (třetí nádvoří) developed in stages after the Great Fire of 1541. Entering through a passage, one is overwhelmed by the presence of **St Vitus' Cathedral** (Katedrála sv Víta), mausoleum of the Kings of Bohemia, a shrine of royal regalia and the metropolitan church of the archdiocese of Prague. The original Romanesque rotunda, to which a triple-naved basilica was added between 1060 and 1096, was built by Prince Wenceslas in the year 929. The present church began life in 1344, when Charles IV, still only heir to the throne, founded a Gothic cathedral on the site to mark the promotion of the bishopric to an archbishopric.

Charles IV intended the cathedral to be one of the most important architectural achievements of his time and hired the prominent French architect Matthias of Arras to supervise its design. After Matthias' death, the work passed to Petr Parléř and later to his sons Wenceslas and John, who between them completed the choir, along with its chapels and the main steeple. All work ceased during the Hussite Wars in the first half of the 15th century. In 1564, the Renaissance dome and parapet were added to the tower by Bonifaz Wohlmut. Nicolo Pacassi created the onion-shaped dome in 1770.

From 1861–1871, Josef Kranner carried out several supplementary building works which were continued by Josef Mocker in 1873. The neo-Gothic western part of the cathedral begun in that year was not completed until 1929 under the supervision of Kamil Hilbert.

The completed cathedral is 124 metres (407 feet) in length, 60 metres (197 feet) wide and 34 metres (111 feet) high. The steeple is over 99 metres (325 feet) high.

Before entering the cathedral walk around the perimeter and observe the various stages of work. On the west façade are statues of Charles IV and 14 saints, created between 1903 and 1908. The central door shows scenes from the history of the construction of the cathedral. The north door portrays scenes from the life of St Adalbert and the south door scenes from the life of St Wenceslas. The bronze doors hanging at all three portals were designed by Vratislav Hugo Brunner and cast by Anýž.

The **Rose Window**, conceived by Prof František Kysela in 1921, is more than 10 metres (33 feet) in diameter and depicts the creation of the world. Portraits of the cathedral architects hang on either side of the window.

The **Golden Portal** (Zlatá brana), built by Petr Parléř in 1367, is set into the south façade. The decorative front wall is a mosaic of coloured stones and gilded glass cubes, created by northern Italian artists. It represents *The Last Judgement* with figures of the Czech patron saints, Charles IV and his consort Eliška Pomořanská. To the east, a covered passage connects the cathedral with the old part of the castle.

As the interior of the cathedral houses 19 separate chapels, each with its own history and notable artwork, the best way to learn about each individual section is to take one of the official guided tours starting at the front of the cathedral.

Above the pillared arcades, a triforium runs around the entire cathedral, its inner parapet decorated with busts of the royal families and those responsible for the building of the cathedral. In front of the neo-Gothic **High Altar**, designed by Josef Kranner between 1868 and 1873, is the white marble **Royal Tomb** created by the Dutch sculptor Alexander Collin (1566–1589). Its reliefs represent Ferdinand I with his consort Anna Jagiello and son Maximilian. The tomb is surrounded by a Renaissance grille by Jiřík Schmidthammer.

To enter the **Royal Crypt** below the tomb, take the stairway leading from the **Chapel of the Holy Rood**. Here you can see remains of the 10th-century rotunda, the Romanesque basilica of the 11th century and the sarcophagi of Charles IV, his children and four consorts plus other Czech kings including Rudolf II.

The main attraction of the cathedral is the beautiful Gothic **Chapel of St Wenceslas** beside the southern transept. A creation of Petr Parléř, the chapel was built on the site of the saint's original grave and in the southern apse of the 10th-century Romanesque rotunda. The frescoes on the walls are encrusted with over 1,300 pieces of jasper, amethyst and gold bezants and portray the Passion cycle and the life of St Wenceslas. Below the window is a small door which leads to the **Treasure Chamber**, resting place of the coronation jewels. The chamber is sealed by seven locks, whose seven keys are kept by seven different institutions. The coronation jewels, including St Wenceslas' crown, are placed on display only on very rare and solemn occasions.

The neo-Gothic main tower of St Vitus' Cathedral

The **Royal Oratory** to the right of the High Altar is decorated with interwoven branches and the initials of King Vladislav Jagiello (1140–1197), who initiated its construction. In the south gallery of the chancel lies the massive silver tomb of St John of Nepomuk, designed by Josef Emanuel Fischer von Erlach in 1736. The three central chapels of the choir, designed by Petr Parléř, contain the Gothic stone tombs of the princes and kings of the Přemyslid dynasty. The Renaissance organ loft, constructed between 1557 and 1561) by court architect Bonifaz Wohlmut, originally marked the end of the choir on the western side, but was moved to its present location in 1924.

Also quite remarkable are the carved wooden reliefs to the north of the High Altar, created in 1630 by the joiner Kašpar Bechteller. They portray the devastation of the cathedral by Calvinists in 1619. In the choir itself is the beautiful statue of the kneeling Cardinal Schwarzenberg, the work of Myslbek (1892–1895). In the cathedral ambulatory are examples of stained glass windows by more recent leading Czech artists including one in the third chapel by Alfons Mucha dating from 1931. To the left of the nave is the controversial 1899 Art Nouveau wooden cross and altar by František Bílek.

The unified design of the buildings lining the southern side of the third courtyard are mere façades covering buildings of a much earlier period: the Renaissance palace of Rudolf II, the early baroque Queen's Palace and the Palace of Maximilian II. The equestrian statue of St George is actually a replica of a 14th-century Gothic sculpture housed in the St George Monastery.

Glance up at the northern side of the courtyard to the huge cathedral steeple towering nearly 100 metres (328 feet) above. In the belfry hang four Renaissance bells, including Zikmund, at 18 tonnes the biggest bell in Bohemia. The tower clock dates from the time of Rudolf II. The upper dial shows the hours, the lower dial the quarter-hours. Unfortunately, the parapet of the steeple tower is now closed to the public. Between the Chapel of St Wenceslas and the steeple is the triple-arched antechamber of the Golden Portal (Zlatá brána) that leads into the transept. The exterior mosaic above the portal depicts the *Last Judgment* and dates from 1370–1371. A vault in the antechamber is fitted with a decorative grille depicting the months according to the zodiac.

The **Royal Palace** (Královsky palác), entered by the stairs near the 1644 baroque Eagle Fountain, dates from the 13th century and served as the seat of the head of state until the 16th century when the Hapsburgs moved their residential quarters to the western part of the castle. Deep below the **Vladislav Hall** (Vladislavský sál) parts of Soběslav's 12th-century palace are still visible. Built by architect Benedikt Ried in Late Gothic style, it was intended as a ceremonial chamber in which to pay homage to the new King Vladislav Jagiello. During the reign of Rudolf II, the Vladislav Hall

Royal Palace

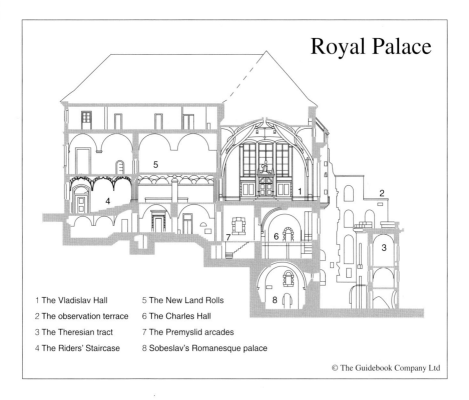

1 The Vladislav Hall   5 The New Land Rolls

2 The observation terrace   6 The Charles Hall

3 The Theresian tract   7 The Premyslid arcades

4 The Riders' Staircase   8 Sobeslav's Romanesque palace

© The Guidebook Company Ltd

was used for social events and elaborate markets of exotic foods and artistic artefacts. Today it is traditionally connected with the election of the President of the Republic.

Turn right at the entrance and continue down a hallway to the **Bohemian Chancellery**. This is situated on the first floor of the Louis Palace and served for two centuries as the office of the Bohemian royal governors. The first room contains a very informative model of the castle as it was in the 18th century. Walk through the Renaissance portal into the smaller assembly room and you will be at the site of the Second Defenestration of Prague, which marked the beginning not only of the Bohemian rebellion but also of the Thirty Years' War. On 23 May 1618, governors Jaroslav Bořita and Vilém Slavata were thrown from the left-hand window for breaking the terms of Rudolf II's Letter of Majesty. The two obelisks in the garden below are said to mark the spots where the two honourable gentlemen landed safely on a dungheap in the castle moat.

Up the spiral staircase in the hall of the **Imperial Court Council** more death sen-

*Riders' Staircase leading to Vladislav Hall, Prague Castle, built
to allow mounted knights to enter the hall for tournaments, c. 1940*

tences were read. During the residence of Rudolf II, and subsequently, the affairs of the Holy Roman Empire were administered from here.

The Vladislav Hall affords access to the choir of the **All Saints' Chapel**, built in the 14th century by Petr Parléř. The present hall was rebuilt after the Great Fire of 1541, and contains several notable works of art: on the High Altar *All Saints* painted by Václav Reiner in 1732; the *Triptych of the Angels* executed by Hans von Aachen in the late 16th century; and the cycle of 12 paintings on the theme of the life of Czech patron saint St Procopius painted by Kristian Dittmann in 1669. The tomb chest near the entrance holds the relics of St Procopius, who died in 1053.

The **Old Diet** (Council Chamber), originally a part of Charles Palace, was rebuilt after the Great Fire by Bonifaz Wohlmut, who copied the Late Gothic rib vault. The chamber was used mainly for sessions of the Supreme Provincial Court and, until 1847, the Estates Diet, assembled here. The royal throne and furnishings are all 19th century.

Situated next to the Old Diet is the **Riders' Staircase** leading down to Vladislav Hall, at one time negotiated on horseback. Part of the Gothic portal dates from around 1355 and came from Charles Palace. Adjoining the portal is the Court of Appeal. The lowest level of the staircase leads to an exhibition of the remains of early 9th-century fortifications.

Nearby is **Mihulka Powder Tower** (Prašná věž), which was built in the late 15th century. The tower formed formed an important feature of the Late Gothic period north fortifications since it enabled defending troops to lay fire across Stag Moat. During the 15th and 16th centuries, it was used as an armoury and munitions store. In the 19th century the tower acquired its popular yet erroneous nickname Mihulka from *mihule* (lamprey) when it was mistakenly identified as the tower featuring a fish pool, used for breeding eels for culinary purposes, that once stood within the castle compound during the 15th and 16th centuries. Inside the tower nowadays is a small museum devoted to the Rudolfine period, when it housed a metal casting foundry and alchemists' laboratory. The heyday of alchemy in Bohemia coincided with the reign of Rudolf II, whose court became a gathering place for famous scholars and scientists like Tycho de Brahe, Johannes Kepler, Jan Jesenius or Tadeáš Hájek, as well as dilettantes and outright confidence tricksters such as Alexander Scott, Filip Jacob Gustenhofer, John Dee and Edward Kelley, who profited from the emperor's interests in arts and science.

On leaving the Royal Palace make your way to St George's Square (Jiřské náměstí), lined on one side by the wing of the Riders' Staircase and the Old Diet. The **Basilica of St George** (Bazilika sv Jiří) and the Benedictine convent form the eastern side of the square. The oldest remaining church building at Prague Castle, the basilica was founded before 920 by Prince Vratislav and contains the remains of Bohemia's first Christian martyr, Princess Ludmila, the grandmother of St Wenceslas, Prince Vratislav and Prince Boleslav II. Concerts are now held here because of the excellent acoustics.

The **Chapel of St John Nepomuk** was built onto the southern wall of the basilica by Kanka between the years 1718 and 1722. In the portal is a statue of Saint George by sculptor Maximilian Brokoff. The altar paintings and dome frescoes are the work of Václav Reiner.

The former **Benedictine Convent** adjoining the basilica houses the **National Gallery of Art**. On exhibition is a collection of Czech art from the 14th to 18th centuries.

The **Black Tower** (Černá věž) formed part of the 12th-century fortifications in which the eastern castle gate was situated. In the mid-13th century, the gate was closed and a new gate built between the tower and the present **Lobkovic Palace**. If you go through this gate you reach the observation terrace and the Old Castle Steps (Staré zámecké schody). Follow the flight of stairs by the House of Czechoslovak Children (Dům Československých dětí) and you will come to **Golden Lane** (Zlatá ulička).

GOLDEN LANE

Wedged into the arches of the Late Gothic fortifications between the **White Tower** (Bílá věž) and **Daliborka Tower** is the area known as Golden Lane. According to legend, Rudolf II's alchemist worked here. In reality, this was where the first castle gunners stayed and later it attracted craftsmen, goldsmiths and tailors. Franz Kafka lived and worked for a time at No 22. More recently the houses have been converted to souvenir and bookshops, and at weekends and in the summer the lane becomes so crowded with tourists that it is practically impassable.

The White Tower was at one time a prison and the 16th-century inscriptions and drawings by prisoners can still be seen on the walls. Daliborka Tower was named after Knight Dalibor, imprisoned in 1498. His fate inspired the Czech composer Bedřich Smetana to write his opera Dalibor.

Follow a passageway from the observation terrace to the gateway leading to the **Castle Gardens** (Hradní zahrada). On summer weekends the southern Castle Gardens, the Garden of Paradise and the Garden on the Ramparts are open to the public and offer a wonderful respite from the crowds. Concerts are performed in the 18th-century music pavilion situated in the Garden on the Ramparts. Josip Plečnik (1872–1957) executed the observation arbour and many other architectural works and sculptures. You can leave from the bastion near the Black Tower or exit out onto Hradčanské náměstí.

THE ROYAL SUMMER PALACE

The **Royal Summer Palace** (Královské letohrádek) located in the Royal Garden, sometimes incorrectly called Belvedere Palace, is said to be the purest example of Italian Renaissance architecture north of the Alps. It was begun in 1538 by King Ferdinand I for his consort Anna after a plan by Paolo della Stella, but was not completed until 1564. The palace is surrounded by an arcaded gallery with rich figural and ornamental relief depicting mythological scenes, historical events and hunting motifs. Also remarkable is the original Renaissance truss designed in the form of a ship's upturned hull and covered in copper plates. In the centre of the Royal Garden is the **Singing Fountain** (Zpívající fontána). Cast in bronze by Tomáš Jaroš after a model by Franceso Terzio of Italy, it takes its name from the sounds made by the falling droplets of water. Continue walking past the Renaissance fig-tree hothouse and on to the southern part of the garden, where there is a magnificent view of the north medieval part of the castle.

Leaving the second courtyard and heading north, you will pass the 17th-century **Riding School of Prague Castle** (Jízdárna Pražského hradu), which has been converted to an exhibition hall of national renown.

The following monuments at Prague Castle are open to the public daily, except Mondays, from 09:00–17:00:

- The Old Royal Palace, the Vladislav Hall, the Old Diet, the Bohemian and the Imperial Chancelleries, Offices of the Nobiliary Quartos of the King dom
- The Romanesque and Gothic Palace with a permanent exhibition *Czechs and Slovaks in Ancient Times*
- St George's Basilica
- St Vitus' Cathedral
- The Treasury
- Prague Castle Gallery
- Golden Lane and Daliborka Tower
- The Powder Tower (Mihulka)

Life changes when they make you a star

'Do you have ration cards for sugar?' the official asked. 'You have to have ration cards for sugar or you can't get a star.'

I didn't particularly care for this star. It was yellow and had a word in a foreign language written in black scraggly letters. It was a poor trade for sugar rations. I needed the sugar to sweeten my fake coffee.

'You needn't worry about your ration card. You only have to show it to me. And from now on you mustn't appear outdoors without the star, I hope I don't have to tell you what would happen to you.'

'You have to stitch down the corners of the star and wear it on the left side, directly on your heart, not any higher or lower. There are very strict regulations about this. You must be wearing the star by tomorrow.'

He handed me a piece of material made of rayon. 'You mustn't get it dirty. Come and get another later. Today we are passing out only one.'

The official had the expression of a busy man who is happy with his work. He had probably been a shop assistant. He must have been glad there was such a demand for his goods.

They were of high quality and cheap, a real bargain. Only one crown for a star made of fine pre-war material. In fact, they were practically giving them away.

I went home and stitched down the tips of the star with a needle and thread. There were six tips and a word on the star, all contorted and twisted, in a foreign language that seemed to make a face at me. I felt for my heart through my coat and marked the place with pins. It beat quite regularly. I looked into the splinter that was my mirror. The black and yellow star looked provocative; it called out for help or screamed in alarm. 'I must get used to going about with this emblem,' I told myself. 'It will probably be difficult. I probably won't be able to slink along the streets as well. People will point their fingers at me.'

I went out the next day. After all, I had to go shopping. I saw people looking at me. At first it seemed as though my shoelaces must be untied or that there was something wrong with my clothes. In some way I had upset the everyday, accepted order of things. I was a sort of blot that didn't belong in the picture of the street and everyone seemed to be aware of this. And I was alone among other people, completely alone, because people would make way for me. They would stop and look at me. I was no longer one of them.

And then I raised my head and became dizzy with a strange feeling. It seemed to me I was no longer even Josef Roubicek, an ordinary bank clerk, one of the many walking about the city. I had become a special person whom everyone looked at and made way for. I was now proud that people were looking at me. Yes, it's me; take a good look. I have the same hands and feet that you do, I'm dressed the way you are, yet I'm different.

'Hello sheriff!' a boy called to me. And everyone laughed, but I knew they weren't laughing at me. I laughed too. It was a funny thing to be going about with this emblem. It was a masquerade that was alien to a world where people worked. It belonged to a fair, to a Punch and Judy show, to somersaults, powdered faces and kicks in the behind.

Jiří Weil, Life With A Star, 1989

Jiří Weil (1900–1959) was one of Central Europe's best known writers in and around the World War II years. Once a militant Communist, he was later expelled from the Party. He translated Marx and Lenin, among others, and wrote several novels, of which Life With A Star *is the most famous.*

Josefov—Jewish Prague

The Old Jewish Town of Prague, situated on a slight slope rising from the right bank of the Vltava, has inspired romantic writers, artists and historians for centuries. The many legends and stories surrounding the area serve to enhance its mysterious intrigue. One story tells of the arrival of the first Jewish settlers, as prophesied by Princess Libuše, founder of Prague. The princess ordered her successor, Duke Hostivit, to welcome the Jews with hospitality, as she foresaw they would provide a blessing for the country. When the Jews did appear at the settlement around Prague Castle at the beginning of the 10th century, the Duke accorded them a generous welcome and permitted them to inhabit Újezd district.

Another legend, which dates from the persecution of the Templar Order, tells of the headless Templar knight who rides through Prague. There are also stories about water spirits who guard many of the dams along the Vltava. And there are the stories of Dr Faustus, who made a pact with the devil in order to turn metal into gold. The devil finally dragged him screaming through the roof of Faustus House. These tales are commonly thought to be based on the colourful figure of the alchemist Mladota, who lived in Prague.

The best loved stories, however, emerged from the mysterious times of Rudolf II and the miracle-working Rabbi Löw. An astronomer and magician, this rabbi is said to have created a creature of mud and clay—the **Golem** (named after the Hebrew word for unformed matter)—which lay dormant until the rabbi uttered the magic word *Shem* and placed the sign of life in the Golem's mouth. According to the story, the creature was supposed to prowl the area to sniff out and prevent crime. One Sabbath eve, Rabbi Löw forgot to remove the sign of life from the mouth of the Golem and the creature went on a rampage. The rabbi was forced to remove the sign forever and the Golem reverted to a heap of mud and clay to lie for eternity under the roof of the Old New Synagogue (Staronová synagóga).

The origin of this legend is based on the first part of the Kabbala, the mystical teachings and writings mentioned in the Talmud. The actual word Golem appears for the first time in the 13th-century commentary of Eliezer ben Yitzhak of Worms. At that time, when Prague was considered one of the centres of Jewish scholarship, the exact instructions for making such a creature were given.

The first Golem was portrayed as the perfect servant, albeit a shade literal in his interpretation of orders. The Golem that evolved by the 16th century was of a more sinister nature, though he too was seen as the protector of the Jewish faith.

The legend of Rabbi Löw, who is said to have visited the banks of the Vltava to gather mud and chant his magic spells, forms the basis of the German novel *Der Go-*

Jewish Town Hall, built in the 16th century and later rebuilt in 1763

lem by Gustav Meyrinck. In 1920, it was made into the first of many films featuring the creation of a man-made being.

The legal status of Jews in Prague and in Bohemia was very favourable until the 12th century. Although considered foreigners, they could move about freely, transact business without limitation and buy land and property. During the 12th century, the Jewish community expanded into the area of the present-day Old New Synagogue.

The situation began to change as a consequence of a number of anti-Jewish regulations promulgated by the Catholic Church, and the Jewish community was segregated from the rest of Staré město by a fortified wall containing six gates, built in 1179 in accordance with the edict of the Third Lantern Council. By the 16th century, any Jews moving into the area were required to settle in the district provided and many restrictions were placed upon them, both in economic and spiritual spheres. The legal status of Jews resident in the Czech Kingdom was codified in 1254 by the royal charter of Přemysl Otakar II. On the one hand it guaranteed legal protection, but on the other it placed them fully under the king's power as *servi camerae*, that is, servants of the royal chamber. In practice it meant that only the sovereign had the right to collect taxes from the Jews, govern Jewish affairs and extend protection when needed.

The charter of Přemysl Otakar II was confirmed by the Luxembourg sovereign Charles IV in 1347. Instead of the promised protection, he exposed the Jews to the bloody pogroms that broke out all over Europe in connection with the immense Black Death epidemic. Jews were widely accused of spreading the plague by poisoning wells in a bid to annihilate the Christians. Some of the biggest pogroms of the Middle Ages occurred in Prague at Easter in 1389 during the reign of Charles' son, Wenceslas IV.

The years 1570–1620 have been called the Golden Age of Prague Jewry and the Prague ghetto, as it was known, underwent rapid growth throughout the 17th century. By the time of the Hapsburg rulers Maximilian and Rudolf II, there were as many as 7,000 Jews living in the narrow network of lanes. Overcrowding became worse and the threat of disease grew.

Emperor Maximilian II (reigned 1564–1576) had cancelled the expulsion decree regarding the Jews of Bohemia and promised the Jews in Prague unlimited and undisturbed residency. His successor Emperor Rudolph II (reigned 1576–1611) granted Prague and Bohemian Jewry many privileges, confirmed their right to live in Prague and the Czech Kingdom, and gave them greater economic freedom.

Conditions in the ghetto reached such a poor level that King Rudolf finally agreed to intervene. His finance minister and first mayor of Jewish Town, Mordechai Markus Maisel (1528–1601), arranged for the demolition of many old buildings, repaving of the streets, construction of the **Jewish Town Hall** and the **Maisel Synagogue** and the establishment of the **Old Jewish Cemetery**. Mordechai Maisel was one of the richest people in Europe at that time and could therefore afford to finance extensive construction work, which substantially changed the character of the area. The street Maiselova was named after the minister in memory of his philanthropic redevelopment schemes.

The plague of 1680 and the destructive fire of 1689, which razed much of the ghetto to the ground, proved heavy setbacks for Jewish Town. The reigns of Emperor Charles VI (1711–1740) and his daughter Maria Theresa (1740–1780) marked the beginning of a very difficult period. Maria Theresa was particularly opposed to the Jewish community and tried to force their expulsion from the country. The situation was further complicated by a second fire in 1754 which gutted many prominent homes and buildings. The damage was so extensive that the community was granted a renewal loan and the town was rebuilt over the next 11 years.

After abortive attempts to reduce the Jewish population to its 1618 level, Charles VI issued the Familial Letters Patent in 1726 and 1727. These effectively limited the number of Jewish families allowed to stay in Bohemia and Moravia. Only the oldest son of a Jewish household could marry legally—other sons could choose between leaving the country or remaining single. The Familial Patent remained in effect, with only partial changes, until 1848.

When Maria Theresa ascended the throne, she promulgated a sanction that guaranteed the reign of the Hapsburgs even through the female line of descent. This sanction caused the Wars for the Habsburg Heritage and, as a result, Austria lost Silesia. Maria Theresa accused the Jews of collaboration with the enemy and, towards the end of 1744, banished the Jews from Prague, Bohemia and Moravia. Only after considerable intervention from England and the Netherlands was the banishment rescinded, and the Jews were permitted to return in 1748.

At the beginning of the 18th century, a prolonged religious controversy raged between the Chief Rabbi of Prague, David Oppenheimer, and his main antagonist, Parson Franciscus Haselbauer. Oppenheimer feared that the Jesuits would confiscate and destroy his extensive collection of Hebrew books and manuscripts and decided to send them to Hannover. In the middle of the 19th century they were bought by the English and today form the core of the Judaica collection of the Bodleian Library in Oxford.

In 1849 negotiations began concerning the incorporation of the Jewish Town, known from 1850 as Josefov, into the covenant of the towns of Prague. In 1861 Josefov became the fifth district of Prague and a massive renewal project was agreed upon. Construction lasted from 1893 until 1917.

Pařížská, which runs from the Old Town Square to the Vltava, was driven through the midst of the old ghetto and created as a tribute to Art Nouveau architecture. Huge areas of the former slum were cleared, though most of the core religious buildings were preserved.

The Jewish community thrived until the approach of World War II, when it was almost completely destroyed in the Nazi Holocaust of 1939, Hitler's final solution to the Jewish problem. Thousands were killed or deported to concentration camps. Those remaining lost their citizenship and became subjects of the state.

The **Old New Synagogue** (Staronová synagóga), located on Pařížská, was one of the first Gothic structures in Prague and is one of the oldest surviving buildings of its kind in central Europe. Originally consisting of a single 13th-century barrel vaulted lower chamber, the building was enlarged by the addition of a double-aisled hall in the last quarter of the 18th century, allowing the segregation of men and women during services. The main decorative symbol unifying the whole conception and design of the main hall is the number 12, symbolizing the 12 tribes of Israel. One seat on the Late Empire benches lining the interior walls is kept empty—this was the seat of the legendary Rabbi Löw and somewhere in the building lie the mud and clay remains of his Golem. The exterior of the rectangular building is plain, with a high saddle roof and a Late Gothic brick gable.

Old Jewish Cemetery, Josefov

The **Jewish Town Hall** (Židovnická radnice) is located at the corner of Červená and Maiselova. It was built in 1586 with funding from Mayor Maisel under the direction of Pankratius Roder. There is a kosher restaurant in the auditorium which draws an international clientele for the set price meal and music. The **High Synagogue** was originally part of the Jewish Town Hall, but in 1883 the way through to the Town Hall was blocked up. The main nave, located on the first floor, has a fine Renaissance ceiling. After the fire of 1689, the synagogue was refurnished with a baroque Torah Ark. Above the united pairs of columns flanking the door to the Ark are the first letters of Psalm 16:8, a paraphrase from the tract *Berakhot*, a crown symbolizing the Torah and quotations from Deuteronomy. The Ark, made in 1690, can be dated by the words *Aron ha-ko-desh* inscribed upon it.

The architect Judah Coref de Herz designed the **Maisel Synagogue** in 1591 and it was built with the permission of the emperor the following year. In his synagogue, Maisel placed a beautiful appliqué Torah curtain, a Torah mantle and his own banner. These objects can be seen in the Prague Jewish Museum, since the original building was destroyed in the fire of 1689. The synagogue was completely rebuilt in baroque style and, after a later fire, was renovated in rococo style.

The fire of 1689 also destroyed a Talmudic school and ritual bath called Klauses. In their place was built the **Klaus Synagogue**, which houses an exhibition of Hebrew manuscripts and old prints, including one of Tycho de Brahe with his silver nose, worn after he lost his own nose in a duel. The building is a combination of several architectural styles: the oldest part of the interior is an exquisite baroque Torah Ark consisting of three separate sections and the vaulted ceiling of the synagogue is decorated with 18th-century rococo stucco. The most recent reconstruction took place in 1883–1884.

The **Old Jewish Cemetery** (Starý židouský hřbitov) is one of the oldest cemeteries in Europe. The exact date of its consecration is not known but the oldest tombstone is dated 1439. Over 12,000 bodies lie here, stacked one on top of another, their tombstones lying in wild disarray. The elaborate inscriptions on many of the tombstones show the name of the deceased, profession and connections with priestly or Levite families (crossed hands) or membership of the tribe of Israel (grapes). The grave of Rabbi Löw bears the symbol of the lion, which is the meaning of his surname in German. An aristocratic coat-of-arms on the gravestone of Hindel Basevi recalls the fact that she was the wife of the first Prague Jew to be awarded noble status. As coffins were not used in those days, bodies were merely wrapped in muslin, facilitating the stacking process. Burials were performed continuously from the 15th century until 1787, when Emperor Joseph II forbade further interments. The last person buried here was Moshe Lipmann Beck.

Among other celebrated figures of the Jewish community buried here are Jehuda Ben Bezalel, the scholar Schelomo Delmedigo, mayor Mordechai Maisel, astronomer David Gans and Rabbi David Oppenheimer.

Through the trees to the southwest is the very moving Renaissance single-nave **Pinkas Synagogue** which now serves as a memorial to the 77,297 Bohemian and Moravian Jews who lost their lives in the Nazi gas chambers. Inscribed on the walls of the interior are 36,000 names with date of birth and date of deportation.

To the right of today's entrance to the cemetery is the **Ceremonial Hall** called Hevra Kaddisha, built in 1906 in pseudo-Romanesque style. Originally it was a meeting place and activities' centre for the members of the Burial Brotherhood Society. After 1926, it became the seat of the pre-war Jewish Museum. On permanent display is a harrowing exhibition of drawings by children sent to Terezín concentration camp.

The last synagogue built in Prague's Jewish Town was the **Spanish Synagogue**, designed in 1868 by V I Ullmann and Joseph Niklas. Its name derives from the square, domed Moorish style and corresponding oriental interior decoration. Until 1939, services were held in the **Cells Synagogue**, a baroque building with a long central hall and barrel vaulting. It was built in 1694 to replace the little cells which served as houses of prayer and classrooms. Today it is used to exhibit old Hebrew manuscripts and printed works.

The **Jewish Museum** in Prague ranks among the oldest and finest institutions of its kind. The idea for the foundation of the Jewish Museum was conceived in 1906 by two men, scientist Dr Salomon Hugo Lieben and municipal councillor and president of the Prague Jewish Community, Dr Augustin Stein. Activities began by gathering Jewish ritual objects. In a relatively short time, they located over 1,000 objects and 1,500 rare books and manuscripts. Among them were an 18th-century circumcision bench, a cradle from the 19th century, stoneware pitchers, glass goblets from the early Burial Brotherhood Societies, numerous silver artefacts such as Torah crowns, shields and pointers, as well as precious Torah curtains and mantles.

In March 1939, the Nazi armies invaded Bohemia and Moravia and introduced many anti-Jewish laws. The communities were abolished and their members gradually deported, then annihilated. At the same time the Nazis ordered the confiscation of all possessions of the Jewish community, synagogue congregations and private individuals. Many of the items were put under the direct control of the Central Jewish Museum, which in turn was controlled by the Central Bureau for Dealing with the Jewish Question. The work of categorizing and qualifying the confiscated items was given to prominent Jewish museologists, who were later murdered. Jewish prisoners in the Central Jewish Museum were primarily engaged in sorting and cataloguing the vast quantities of items and in creating impressive exhibitions.

After the annihilation of most museum employees at the end of 1944, all expert activities ceased and the museum became a mere storehouse. The Central Jewish Museum was not open to the public and a certain death sentence awaited those assigned to a job there. Though the workers tried valiantly to maintain a method of establishing proper ownership after the war, their efforts were mostly in vain as so few Jews from Moravia and Bohemia survived.

In 1946, after the liberation of Prague, the Council of Jewish Communities attempted to revive the museum—which contained over 30,000 artefacts and 100,000 library volumes—and open a few exhibitions. However, the population was so depleted it was soon obvious they had neither the strength nor the means to continue and the collection was turned over to the Czechoslovak State.

The Jewish Museum currently houses one of the world's greatest collections of Judaica, both artistic and folkloric. Tickets for all exhibitions may be purchased from the High Synagogue, opposite the entrance to the Old New Synagogue in Červená.

Art Nouveau Movement

The mid-19th century was a period of rapidly changing trends in art and architecture. During the 1870s, French Impressionists scandalized the art world with their interpretations of light and shadow. Cubism, Fauvism and Expressionism followed, not only in art, but in architecture and the creation of everyday household items.

With the development of new construction technology, based primarily on the use of cast iron, steel and glass, the world experienced an entirely new concept of building, concretized in such structures as the Crystal Palace and the Eiffel Tower. These avant-garde styles came to represent the progressive new age.

In keeping with this modern thinking, artists began experimenting with new themes. A preference for natural lines and curves evolved and a re-creation of stylized flora and fauna provided the basis for the typical new style, which became known as **Art Nouveau.**

Art Nouveau developed into a universal style and became the expression of Czech society of that time. It reproduced motifs of Czech history, enhancing the ideals of revival in a nation living under the Austrian Hapsburg monarchy. Prague was endeavouring to overcome its provincial image and to equal neighbouring Vienna in stateliness and social stature.

The 1890s were marked by great public activity and the arrival of a new political and culturally strengthened generation anxious to see the rebirth of Czech nationalism. The architectural bible of the age, *Manifesto of the Modernists (Manifest Moderny);* was published in 1895. In 1896, the *Art Nouveau Almanac* was published by S K Neumann, in which he attacked the establishment and criticized the banality of daily existence.

To mark the centenary of industrialization, Prague was host to the 1891 Jubilee of the Kingdom of Bohemia, modelled on the French World Exhibition in Paris. Architect Bedřich Munzberger built the Industrial Palace on the exhibition grounds, using glass and steel as primary materials. The **Hanavský Pavilion**, a magnificent period example using pseudo-Renaissance iron castings, was later moved to its present location at the top of Letná Hill. It now houses a colourful disco and café and is a favourite with locals. The observation tower on Petřín Hill, a smaller model of the Eiffel Tower in Paris, was also built for the Jubilee.

When **Alfons Mucha**'s innovative poster for the *Gismonda* drama appeared in Paris in 1895, he presented Sarah Bernhardt to her public in a novel way.

The first Art Nouveau building, even though not in the purest form of the style, was **Café Corso**—no longer in existence—built in 1897 on Na příkopě. It was designed by architect Friedrich Ohmann, who taught at the Prague College of Applied Arts.

Municipal House, Na příkopě

Peterkův dům, on Wenceslas Square, is one of Prague's finest Art Nouveau buildings. It is the work of Jan Kotera and was built in 1890. The building introduced a new concept of the apartment house with a tri-axial ground floor plan connecting private and public spaces. It is decorated with ornamental stucco details of natural plant motifs on a pastel façade.

Many buildings in the Art Nouveau style are characterized by their plant motif ornamentation, representing tree branches or vines with stylized fruit or flowers. Interior designs constitute bold stained or etched glass panels, and lavish ironwork on staircases and balconies.

The easiest building to locate, and most symbolic of the period, is the **Evropa Hotel** on Wenceslas Square. The larger-than-life asymmetric façade is covered with large floral ornaments and a wealth of fine mosaic detail. It was designed and built in 1903–1904 by two of Ohmann's disciples, Alois Dryak and Bedřich Bendelmayer. These two architects also designed the **Central Hotel** on Hybernská. Another classic hotel example is the beautifully restored **Hotel Palace** on Jindřišská.

Prague's **Main Railway Station** (Hlavní nádraží), built between 1901–1909, was the creation of Josef Fanta and is considered one of his greatest achievements. The central pavilion is decorated with a glazed portal and two traditional towers. The tracks are protected by the vast glass-roofed hangar structures.

Stroll down **Masaryk Embankment** (Masarykovo nábřeží) and visit a living museum of Art Nouveau architecture. Many buildings, like Hlahol Choir at No 24, are adorned with massive, intricately tiled mosaics. The former Zajištóvací Bank, at the corner of Na Struze, is one of several buildings ornamented with dramatic sculptures by Ladislav Saloun.

U Nováků, on Vodičkova near Wenceslas Square, is a fine example of stained glass and metal combination. It was built by architect Osvald Polívka in Late Historicism style. The creator of the façade mosaic was painter Jan Preisler and is based on folklore motifs executed in delicate colours: its most notable elements are a large, colourful peacock and a relief of a greyhound. Polívka became one of Prague's leading exponents of Art Nouveau and produced other prominent works on Národní and Na příkopě, site of his principle contribution, **Municipal House** (Obecní dům).

Municipal House is the combined work of Osvald Polívka and Antonín Balsánek. The foyer and lofty cupola open into spacious single-storey wings. In the core of the house is one of Prague's most treasured concert halls, bearing the name of Bedřich Smetana, the 19th-century Czech composer. The façade was decorated by sculptors Ladislav Saloun and Josef Maratka, the halls and salons by painters Jan Preisler, Josef Palacký, Alfons Mucha and Max Švabinský. Karel Špillar created the remarkable exterior mosaic, which is an apotheosis of the city.

More of Polívka's work can be seen on the two adjacent buildings of the former **Land Bank** (Živnostenská bank). The left-hand building was built in 1894–1896 and the right-hand one in 1911 upon the completion of the Municipal House. The detailed interior and stucco façade decorations are by Celda Kloucek and Jan Preisler. Mikoláš Aleš designed the mosaics and Max Švabinský the typically Art Nouveau murals in the vestibule of the first building.

From the Municipal House, walk into the **Old Town Square**, a gem of Gothic and baroque architecture, but also an Art Nouveau showcase. The building now housing the Ministry of Trade was designed by Polívka in 1900. It is a rather amusing combination of Renaissance and baroque lines, decorated with Art Nouveau sculptures by František Procházka, Ladislav Saloun and Bohuslav Schnirch.

In the centre of the Old Town Square is the **Monument to Jan Hus** by Ladislav Saloun, unquestionably the best known Art Nouveau sculpture in the Czech Republic.

Other remarkable Art Nouveau buildings in downtown Prague include the corner house No 1/761 on **Jungmann Square** (Jungmannovo náměstí), built in 1906, with a lavishly designed façade and original circular door, and the gilt embellished **Dorfler House**, No 7/391, built in 1905, on Na příkopě. There are also good examples on **Kaprora**, **Maiselova** and **Široká** utilizing incredible bas-relief stucco designs.

Prague bridges did not miss the Art Nouveau movement. Both metal spanning sections and lighting are highly decorative. A good example is the **Svatopluk Čech**

Bridge at the end of Pařížská. Built in 1905, it was designed by Jiří Soukup in collaboration with architect Jan Koula. Be sure to peer over the side at the elegant sculptural decorations and gilded sunburst lamps. Crossing the Vltava from the National Theatre will take you across the stone **Legions Bridge** (most Legii), built in 1899–1901. Designer Antonín Balšánek created in harmony with the theatre and it is adorned with several Art Nouveau sculptural decorations.

Pařížska has the most unified design. Following the large scale clearing of the Jewish ghetto, the street was created as an Art Nouveau showpiece and soon became a focal point of architectural study. Many of the houses nearest the Inter-Continental Hotel incorporate a Jewish theme.

A competition was held to design a statue in commemoration of one of Prague's outstanding historians and politicians, František Palacký, author of the authoritative *History of the Czech Nation in Bohemia and Moravia*. The winner of the competition, Stanislav Sucharda, took 13 years to finish his work. The statue, **Palacký Monument** on Palackého náměstí, combines many Impressionistic elements with the gentle sweeping lines typical of Art Nouveau and the symbolism of the work is one familiar to the Czech psyche. The central figure of Palacký expresses restraint and dignity, the groups around him and the figures on the two pylons represent the two periods of Czech history: the pagan and the Hussite. Great attention to detailed facial expressions conveys the intensity of the movement. Allegorical figures such as Oppression, the Awakener and Victory are also represented.

Another outstanding Art Nouveau sculptor and designer native to Prague was František Bílek, who was heavily influenced by religion, literary and artistic symbolism, and mysticism. His most famous work was the carved wooden **Crucifixion** created in 1897 for St Vitus' Cathedral. Its sweeping lines and powerful impact are considered by some the finest of the period. Another of his works, the 1905 **Statue of Moses**, stands opposite the Old New Synagogue on Pařížská. Bílek's home on Mickiewicz near the Royal Summer Residence also warrants a visit.

Though the Art Nouveau movement has its critics, it has contributed as much as any architectural style to the overall beauty of Prague. Today, the Art Nouveau buildings and other works of art give an insight into the dynamic turn-of-the-century Bohemian lifestyle that would otherwise go unnoticed and forgotten.

Alfons Mucha

Alfons Mucha, born in southern Moravia in 1860, joined other artist compatriots in Paris in an effort to enhance his skills and to attain a more European flavour. He mostly sought the company of Vojtech Hynais and Václav Brožík and also became friends with Paul Gauguin and members of the Les Nabis group. Mucha gained fame throughout the world, not only for his decorative panels and posters but also for his window glass and jewels, furniture, vessels, textiles and carpets. Today many unassuming Prague flats have exquisitely etched glass door panels signed by Mucha. The sad fact is that many go unnoticed and unappreciated.

Mucha travelled and lived abroad for much of his creative life returning to live in Czechoslovakia only in 1913. He considered one of his greatest contributions to be the painted decorations of the **Municipal House** in Prague. Despite varying degrees of quality in the construction, the building and its interior constitute a monument to one stage in the development of Czech art.

In his studio at Zbiroh Château, Mucha began to work on the first canvas of the Slav Epic Cycle. In 1918, he designed the Czechoslovakia State Emblem, the first Czechoslovakian stamps and banknotes. In the following year art lovers from all over the world admired the first 11 canvases of his Slav Epic Cycle when they were exhibited at the Klementinum. On 1 September 1928, the completed cycle of 20 monumental canvases was exhibited in Prague. His work was influenced by symbolism, which he made his own by the use of distinctive, elegant and decorative lines. In 1931, he designed a stained-glass window, *The Work of Slav Missionaries,* for the new archbishop's chapel in St Vitus' Cathedral. This was his last major finished work before his death in 1939. He is buried on Vyšehrad Hill in Prague.

Poster by Alfons Maria Mucha, designed for an exhibition at the
Société Populaire des Beaux Arts

History of the Prague Coffee House

Though few Czechs would find much favour with the Hapsburg emperors or Ottoman Turks today, they will concede a small debt to one of the city's most popular beverages, coffee, and its second most entrenched institution, the coffee house. In fact it was an Armenian, Deodat Damajan, who was granted a license to 'brew and dispense the Turkish drink', and who founded Prague's first coffee house in 1714.

There was a time when Prague, as the cultural centre of the world, was a city as full of coffee houses as Vienna or Paris. Great thinkers of decades past have often described the coffee house as a way of life or more elaborately as an entire life philosophy. In any event, in Prague most social life revolved around them with each one attracting its own group of regulars, usually people with similar interests or professions. Waiters were more like friends and confidantes. Artists, journalists and prim, white-gloved ladies mingled with actors, dramatists and world travellers. Many a patron used the coffee house as a place to study, conduct business or even as a permanent mailing address.

Orson Welles once described the coffee house as 'the only place in the world where you can sit unmolested for eight hours or longer, drink but a single cup, and still be treated like a king'. Coffee was the least important element of the entire affair, it was merely the price paid for admission to a place where one could choose to be alone in the company of others.

It was that very element of convivial camaraderie which spelled the death sentence for many a coffee house in Prague, especially after World War II when the Communist government became highly suspicious of the free-wheeling nature of the conversation they inspired. Most of the large coffee houses were closed, leaving the remaining few to serve a carefully watched clientele.

Even though that glorious heyday has long passed and the new capitalists are hardly likely to smile on a business which encourages the customer to linger for hours over a single 20 kčs purchase, some coffee houses are well worth visiting.

The last of the large and important coffee houses is the **Café Slávia** (Národní 1), which opened its doors in 1863, around the same time as the National Theatre just across the street. The Great Slávia, as it was called, is housed in the former Lažanský Palace designed by architect Vojtěch Ignác Ullmann. It was closed temporarily in 1993 and sold to American developers, who are due to reopen it soon.

Planned originally as a meeting place for Bohemia's élite set of actors, writers, musicians and composers, plus a thriving congregation of theatre students, it was not opened officially as a café until 1881. After that time there was no looking back. The list of famous people who have whiled away their hours over the Slávia's strong black brew is endless: writer Karel Čapek, composer Antonín Dvořák and painter Jan Zrzavý were all once regulars. It is even claimed that much of the new government was planned by the country's most famous playwright and his colleagues over many thoughtfully contemplated cups of coffee at the Slávia.

Poets also frequented the Slávia and, in that brief, glorious period between the two world wars it even lured the crowds from Vienna. Nobel prize-winner Jaroslav Seifert was a regular in his younger days and his circle of fellow poets included Jiří Wolker and Vítěslav Nezval. After Wolker's death, his mother held a wake in his honour, during which she propped up a picture of her son and ordered absinthe, Wolker's favourite drink, to be served to all.

Singers and actors still appear after the occasional performance across at the National. And the Great Ladies, those fading roses who are the widows of factory owners from the First 'Golden' Republic, still wander in to hold court. Students of art and film come from the nearby faculties of Charles University. But these days it is the well-heeled tourists and foreign students who make up most of the clientele, who come to see and be seen by Prague's new breed of yuppies. For as with all Prague institutions, prices at the Slávia are keeping pace with the West.

Extensive renovations hit the Slávia in the early 1980s, when it was closed for several years. The work carried out by architect Jan Fišer seemed to meet universal approval when it reopened on 18 November 1983. The foyer statue is a creation by Krištůfek, the frescoes on the ceiling are by Riedlbauch and the distinctive light fixtures are pure Fišer.

The coffee, of course, is still pure Slávia and comes in a number of varieties: Viennese, Turkish, Ruskě and cappuccino among them. Wine, liquor and bottled beer are also available. There is a small daily selection of slightly dry sandwiches and pastries plus some of the best ice cream in town. Open daily from 08:00 to midnight.

Another *grande dame* of the coffee house clique is the **Hotel Evropa** on Wenceslas Square, a living museum of some of the finest Art Nouveau architecture in the world. According to the writer Jaroslav Seifert, the waiters visited the barber's twice daily to be shaved. Today the coffee shop is a bit down at heel, but sit back and listen to the ageing trio playing their slightly off-beat music and you will easily imagine it as it once was.

Other famous coffee houses include: another unbeatable Art Nouveau classic, the **People's House** (Obecní dům) at náměstí Republiky; Kafka, Kisch and the 'Arconaut' circles frequented the **Café Arco** at Hybernská 16. You can also try: **Columbia**, Staroměstskě náměstí 15; **Kajetánka**, Hradčany, Kajetánská zahrada; **Malostranská Kavárna**, Malostranskě náměstí 28; **Mysák**, Vodičkova 31; **Praha**, Václavskě náměstí 10; **Savarin**, Na příkopě 10; and **U Slatěho Hada**, Karlova.

STALIN FOR AUCTION

The Czechs had no Berlin Wall. The rolled bails of wire from the former Iron Curtain have not met with much commercial appeal. However, the industrious people of Kamorov hit on what they predicted to be the sale of the century . . . the auction of their 3.2-metre (10.5-foot) sandstone statue of Generalissimo Josef Stalin.

The story began in the early 1950s, when a statue of Josef Stalin took eighteen months to become reality in June 1951. At a stroke, the old town park disappeared; old trees vanished; bushes and paths melted into thin air. Citizens volunteered thousands of hours to the project. It was a joint effort by all Kamorov to create a work of art to proclaim for eternity their unbreakable friendship with Stalin.

On the day the statue was unveiled the wave of Communist enthusiasm was overwhelming. The number of volunteer workers had been increased to include practically the whole town. The District National Committee planned the usual ceremonies with rousing speeches, flamboyant presentations and well-orchestrated rallies. School children paraded with colourful banners and bonfires were lit throughout the evening.

Although the local inhabitants had built and financed the statue with their own sweat and hard-earned money, as with most works of art in the former East Bloc, it eventually became the property of the State.

Similar statues were created across much of Eastern Europe, and over the years most were destroyed or just disappeared. In time, the statue in Kamorov became the focus of hatred, which gradually faded to disregard. Their disdain was such that they could not even be bothered to destroy it.

After the Velvet Revolution, the statue once again became a treasured item—this time because of what it could bring to the newly capitalistic people of Kamorov in the way of financial reward. When they realized the monetary value of the statue, it was carefully removed to the local depository. The Ministry of Culture delegated Artia, a foreign trade corporation, as the official dealer with the Western market. The citizens of Kamorov suggested a price of US$100,000, though secretly felt they would be happy with half that amount.

Despite much predictable squabbling with the local National Committee and the refusal of Sotheby's London office to handle the sale, bids began pouring in from all over the world. One offer of $80,000 cash plus $80,000 in medical equipment for the local hospital came from a private bidder in far-off Florida. Other bids, with varying degrees of seriousness, flooded in from all over Europe.

Though neither the final sale price, nor even the location of the highest bidder have been announced, it has been noted with delight that quite a few very pleasant changes have taken place in the community of Kamorov.

Removal of Prague's 30-metre-high statue of Stalin, whose sculptor Otakar Svec shot himself in 1954 before completion of the piece

Beer and Pubs

Every Czech notes with pride that their beer brewing heritage dates back to the early 11th century, but it was not until the art was perfected by the Pilsner brewery in 1842 that the reputation spread world-wide. Since then pubs have become an integral part of Czech social life and culture.

Pre-revolution Prague pubs were all state-owned and, with the exception of a few, were fairly standard smoke-laden dens filled with animated conversation and good beer. Tables and chairs were stark and uncomfortable, walls were covered with drab wooden panels and the decorations consisted of the prerequisite Socialist paintings of smiling, happy workers.

There has been good news and bad since 1989. Along with privatization has come not only streamlining and up-market décor changes, but also a huge increase in prices and the inevitable closing of many pubs. What used to be the ultimate blending of classes is now available only to the upwardly-mobile and pub crawling tourists. Waiters once unbothered about how long a customer lingered over his brew are now learning the financial realities of customer turnover much faster than they are learning about good service.

Pubs, however, are still the best way to get a real feel for Prague and it is well worth plucking up the courage to venture into one. As few offer the intimacy of tables for two, you will be thrust into a group of four, six or even more, where conversation is likely to be in as many different languages.

Menus are quite simple and usually appear scribbled on a large wooden board. Pubs are so noisy you can usually just point as you will probably get some form of the national dish—goulash and dumplings—anyway. The taste is great but forget about counting calories! This is the home of not-so-lean cuts of pork or beef served in a rich, golden brown gravy with thick white *knedle*, as the Czechs call their form of dumpling. It looks more akin to slabs of crustless white bread rather than the usual dough balls, but it is equally heavy to digest. Cutlery is plonked in the middle of the table *en masse* leaving the customer to fend for himself.

Salads and vegetables are a bit thin on the ground but you can get the occasional sliced cucumber soaked in sweetened water. There are also platters of luncheon meats and pungent cheeses served with giant wedges of crusty bread.

In any case, it is neither the food nor the decoration that makes the pub, but the beer. And that must be perfect—fresh, cold, with a good thick head that does not collapse straight away, pulled from draught taps that are cleaned regularly. The worst strike to threaten the newly independent Czechoslovakia in 1990 occurred when Budvar announced its plan to put beer in cans—a move constituting heresy to most Czechs.

U Kalicha pub, long associated with Josef Hašek

You will know immediately if you are in a local pub as foreigners and women tend to be scarce. Czechs are friendly enough but they have been known to stare rather more openly than one might find comfortable. There is a good selection of pubs with mixed clientele though, so you should not have difficulty finding a pub to call your own.

U **Fleků** (Křemencova 11, Prague 1) is a mandatory stop for tourists, beer lovers or not. The original malt house and brewery were established in 1459. It has its own 450-seat outdoor garden where Czech bands perform all summer. The courtyard is filled with reliefs of medieval knights in action and odd bits of equipment from the early days of the brewery.

There are several dining rooms, all with wooden-beamed ceilings, iron chandeliers and stained glass windows. Meals consist of goulash jazzed up with a serving of rice or sometimes potatoes. Menus in English—normally a rare sight—are available, giving an indication of the pub's tourist leanings. Despite this, U Fleků is best known for its dark 13° beer, Flekovský ležák, made only for this pub in the brewery next door. An experience you'll never forget if, indeed, you remember it the next day!

Beer was also brewed until 1953 at U **Tomáše** pub (Letenská 12, Prague 1). Just a short walk from Charles Bridge, the brewery was established by Augustine monks in 1352 and named after the neighbouring St Thomas Church. Today the strong dark 12° beer comes from the Bráník brewery and the cavernous basement pub is always filled with regulars from nearby Charles University and plenty of tourists.

The beer has a distinctly sweet taste with a strong malty aftertaste. It complements perfectly the Goulash St Thomas, a fiery version of the national dish with sausage and a garnish of red hot pepper.

In summer there is an outdoor barbecue on a huge open fire serving grilled sausages, pork and chicken, whose mouth-watering aroma will help you locate the pub from blocks away.

The traditions of the U **Supa** pub (The Vulture, Čeletná 22, Prague 1) go back to the 14th century. Here you can sip the 14° brew known as Speciál bráník under medieval arched ceilings.

Slightly off the beaten path is **U Palivce** (Fýgnerovo náměstí 1), a small, cosy establishment where they serve succulent roast duck and *knedle* in a thin flavourful natural gravy. The interior was renovated around the turn of the century with wonderful period advertising and a well-used upright piano. The beer served is the world famous Pilsner Urquell which the Czechs call Prazdroj.

At **U zlatého tygra** (The Golden Tiger, Husova 17, Prague 1) they have been serving 12° Pilsner Urquell since 1842. Another well known Pilsner Urquell watering hole, **U Pinkasů** on Jungmannovo náměstí No 15, near Wenceslas Square, is where locals have been drinking for 148 years.

Near Prague Castle on Loreta Square stands a very pretty pub, **U černěho vola** (The Black Ox), where the speciality is 12° Velkopopovice served with enormous German sausages and crusty mustard-covered slabs of brown bread. Not far away is Nerudova, a street full of pubs and wine restaurants. The best known pub, **U Bonaparta**, serves the 12° Smíchov beer. Locals swear that the best Pilsner Prazdroj is on tap at **U dvou koček** (The Two Cats), at Uhelný trh 10.

The most famous pub of all has to be **U Kalicha** (The Chalice, Na bojišti 12, Prague 2), haunt of the famous Czech writer Jaroslav Hašek, who wrote **The Good Soldier Švejk**. Švejk is to the Czech character as *mañana* is to the Spanish and it is most useful to understand it. The rogue-like Švejk lived his fictional life during World War I, when he bungled his way through a million scrapes with nonsensical behaviour and a mask of clownishness.

Though his adventures were supposedly only in Hašek's imagination, the pub Švejk loved really exists and was Hašek's creative source. The walls are covered with hand-written messages from the Good Soldier and other souvenirs from his life.

PUB ETIQUETTE

- Sometimes the waiter will point out an empty spot as you enter but if not, sit wherever there is an empty seat. If there are others at the table ask, *Je tu volno?* Is anyone sitting here?
- The Czech word for beer is *pivo*, but all you have to do is place a coaster in front of you to indicate you would like a beer.
- Service may not be prompt so be patient. Waving frantically or whistling will definitely not endear you to the waiter and it could easily increase the tab.
- The waiter keeps track of your bill by marking ticks on the coaster or a small piece of paper. He will tally it up when you have finished drinking.
- When you are ready to pay, say *Platit, prozím*. A different waiter usually handles the money. In general Czech tips are low, usually just rounded up to the nearest whole number and seldom more than a few crowns, though ten per cent is considered quite generous.

The Pursuit of Entertainment

Although Prague has changed considerably over the past decade, its metamorphosis has not been phoenix-like. Instead it has been the transition of a butterfly emerging from a forty-year-old cocoon. The butterfly is still beautiful but its wings are stiff and its first attempts at flight are clumsy.

One of the most obvious changes in Prague is the burgeoning league of entrepreneurs. The free market economy in the Czech Republic has unleashed a long-stifled creativity. Wenceslas Square, the main thoroughfare, is crowded with street vendors selling everything from Western newspapers to hand-crafted jewellery. You can even buy wacky computer horoscopes, or the wildly popular board game Stalin, based on the game of Monopoly.

Nightlife is not one of Prague's strong points and standards are well below current Western ideas of entertainment although there has been an explosion of cafés, restaurants and bars in recent years. The price paid for decadent capitalism is the emergence of a huge market exploiting 40 years of State puritanism. What started as a dirty joke has turned into a national movement. The Independent Erotic Initiative, a political party, was established in 1990 with 3,500 members and has grown beyond all imagination. One of the party's aims was to fight for the right to show erotic films and to scrap the old, strictly controlled laws on public decency.

Striptease too came to Prague with lightning speed. The first houses of artistic dance opened on Wenceslas Square only months after the Velvet Revolution. At first the advertisements to recruit dancers had little pull, but once the dollar signs flashed up, competition among dancers became keen.

Gambling, which was stamped out by the Communists in 1949, is currently experiencing a strong resurgence. The casinos that have opened all across the country aim to provide a more upscale form of entertainment for tourists, but an interesting new breed of high rollers is developing amongst residents. Society-seeking locals still prefer wine bars and coffee houses to the tragic mishmash of discos, popular among lambada enthusiasts and prostitutes. Discos in Prague were once considered the sole haunts of the young Communist élite and still have a certain undesirable stigma. The only tolerable dancing spot at present is at **U bilého koníčka** on Staroměstské nám 20, or you could try **Radost FX** at Bělehradská 120 or **Larka** on Charles Bridge, towards Staré město. Younger subcultures do not like dancing much and usually congregate at places like **Újezd**, on Újezd 18, a baroque hovel over a Romanesque cellar. Here you can listen to rampant bands squealing into the wee hours of the morning.

For a more sedate evening you could try **Bohemian Fantasy**, touted as a musical journey through the Czech Republic with food. Stop by Lucerna, Štěpánská 61 (off Wenceslas Square), for information and tickets. Another new spectacular is **The Krizik Fountain** at Prague's Exhibition Grounds, advertised as 'an imaginative musical on the theme of Shakespeare's *A Midsummer Night's Dream*'.

The best way to find out what is happening on a particular night is to check the visitor's guide section in one of the English language newspapers.

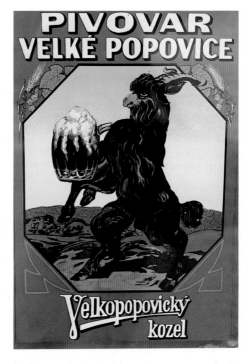

Enamel beer sign

Outside Prague

If you are planning to spend more than a few days in Prague, why not venture outside the city centre and sample some of the historic sites in the surrounding countryside (see map page 154). Čedok has provided the following suggestions.

Day Trips

TROJA CHÂTEAU

The site of present day Troja was originally occupied by the villages of Zadní Ovenec and Horní Ovenec, mentioned in documents as early as 1197. In the 18th century the community was renamed Troja after the château and later expanded into a garden city.

Built in the 17th century for Count Vaclav Vojtěch Šternberg and his wife Klára, Troja Château has been brilliantly restored to its original beauty. It is considered to be the work of Jean Baptiste Methey—although current research indicates that the creator of this grandiose structure may have been Prague architect Dominico de Orsini—and was conceived as a summer residence for its owner. After ten years of reconstruction, the château was officially reopened to the public in 1989 as an outstanding cultural and historical centre of Prague's artistic and social life.

The entire complex is made up of 20 structures, including the original stables and other outbuildings. The château itself has three wings, dominated in front by a garden and a monumental staircase leading to the first floor. The staircase is richly decorated with statues depicting mythical scenes, the work of Dresden sculptors J J and P Heermann. Baroque vases and busts adorn the park terraces.

The interior of the château houses residential quarters, a chapel with wall paintings by F and G Marchetti and a large ballroom, with ceiling and wall paintings by the Dutch painter Abraham Godin. The paintings, on themes from ancient mythology and the glorification of Hapsburg expoits against the Turks, have been restored to their original beauty by members of the Czech Artists Fund.

A new brilliance has also been given to the original baroque garden with the addition of a small outdoor theatre, whose twin stages are used for holding various cultural events. Concerts are held on the garden staircase.

A permanent exhibition of Czech paintings and sculpture of the 19th century and a collection of Czech baroque cut glass are housed in the château. Part of the former stables have been converted into a stylish restaurant offering excellent refreshments for visitors.

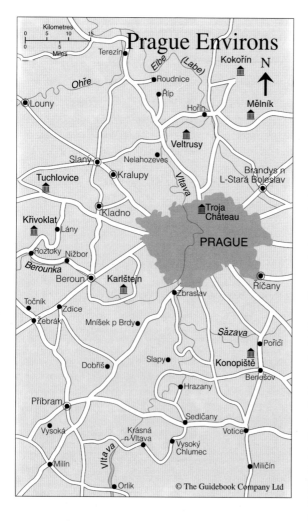

Prague Environs

THE ZOOLOGICAL GARDENS

The Zoological Gardens (Zoologická zahrada) are located just across the street from Troja Château. Few zoological gardens have meadows, gorges, slopes, woods and rocks like this one, where the animals have plenty of greenery and a natural environment. The zoo at Troja was opened in 1931. It covers an area of 45 hectares (111 acres) and accommodates some 2,000 animals of 600 different species.

The specialty are the Przewalski horses, the wild antecedents of the domestic horse, which are extinct in their natural environment. The breeding programme is one of the Zoo's biggest successes. The Zoological Gardens are open daily throughout the year and can be reached by taking a tram to the Osadní stop in Holešovice and then a bus.

KARLŠTEJN

Commissioned by Charles IV in the 14th century, Karlštejn Castle was built to house the royal jewels. The impressive fortress sits atop a hill overlooking a quaint village. Enjoy a walk through the meadows and a sundae in one of the little shops afterwards.

There is a guided tour of the reconstructed interior, but you may opt to miss it. To get there, take a direct train from Smíchov on metro line B—the journey takes about one hour. Then wander up through the town to the castle.

KONOPIŠTĚ

The château once owned by the ill-fated Archduke Franz Ferdinand offers peacock-filled gardens, bears in moats, beautiful woods and a peaceful lake. Despite over-antlered walls, designed as hunting prizes for the archduke, Konopiště's interior is more appealing than Karlštejn's. The guided tour, when in a language you understand, gives you insight into the early goings-on at the old château. To get there, take the train to Benešov from Hlavní nádraží, walk across the tracks and follow the signs to Konopiště. There is a welcoming restaurant there as your reward. Konopiště is closed on Mondays.

TEREZÍN

This is a much grimmer sort of visit. A late baroque fortress, it was used as a Nazi concentration camp where 35,000 Jews died. It is about one hour from Prague and can be reached by bus. Contact Čedok (tel 212 71 11) or Wittmann Tour (tel 25 12 35) for information.

Tours

SOUTH MORAVIA

The South Moravian wine region, located south of Brno, makes a leisurely two-to-three day trip from Prague. The region's vineyards are very close to those of Austria's Weinviertel in the wind-blown loess of the Danube valley. In all, over 20 million gallons of wine are produced in the Czech Republic, though most of it remains unknown in the Western world as virtually none is exported.

At the centre of the region is the charming old town of Mikulov, with its impressive 13th-century château, inspiring the Gothic church of St Wenceslas and many buildings and monuments in Renaissance or baroque style. You can climb the hills behind the town for a panoramic view of the vines that have made the area famous for centuries.

To make the most of your time in the region, you should visit one of the wine villages such as Petrov-Plzeň, near the town of Hodonín. This is a tiny community of little blue and white cellars, grouped along a tree-lined dirt road. In early spring tourists are few and the atmosphere relaxed, but in summer the little village is alive with

Mozart's Bertramka

Tucked away up the winding road on the way to Smíchov is **Bertramka**, the villa once shared by Wolfgang Amadeus Mozart and Dušek and his wife. Bertramka was built on the site of a vintner's house at the turn of the 17th century by the wealthy Smíchov brewer J Pimskorm, as a small summer palace. It was named after its former owner, F Bertramsky, and enlarged during reconstruction in classical style in the latter half of the 18th century.

Bertramka's acme covered the years 1784 to 1799, when it served as the Dušek's summer dwelling. Piano virtuoso and composer, F Dušek and his wife Josefa, a well-known singer, invited guests from the musical world and organized frivolous picnics with musical productions. Mozart stayed at Bertramka on two different occasions and it was here that he completed his opera *Don Giovanni*, whose première took place on 29 November 1787 at the Nostic (now Týl) Theatre.

In later years, the villa Bertramka fell into disuse, and in 1925 its last owner bequeathed it to the Mozarteum Foundation in Salzburg. In 1927 a Mozart Community was founded in Prague and purchased Bertramka. In the 1950s the homestead was taken over by the music department of the National Museum and in 1956, in honour of the 200th anniversary of Mozart's birth, it was renovated in order to serve as a museum and memorial to the Dušeks and Mozart.

At the beginning of 1986, the building was closed and the exhibits removed to make way for renovations which were painstakingly carried out over the next year. The house was provided with insulation against damp and a new pantile roof. The lighting was changed and an exterior platform built. Employees of the Arts and Crafts Centre restored all the paintwork to its original state, imbuing the ceiling in Mozart's bedroom with new life. Other exhibits were introduced and the barn and hayloft in the adjoining garden underwent reconstruction.

Interiors partly preserved from the time of Mozart's sojourns are supplemented with period furniture and mementos from the play *Amadeus*. In the hall stand a hammer piano and a harpsichord with decorated keys—instruments on which the composer played. Apart from unique materials such as sheet music and period copies of Mozart's works, envelopes containing

Mozart's hair and a number of portraits, there is an exhibition of photographs bringing to life the composer's walks through Prague.

Some of Prague's most delightful chamber music concerts are given in the beautifully restored *sala terrena*. Events from the Prague Spring Music Festival are conducted at Bertramka, as are some of the competitions held for young musicians. At the end of the summer the garden is opened to young fashion designers for a presentation of garments, jewellery and fashion accessories.

Poster advertising a Mozart festival at the east gate of
Prague Castle

Krakonoš
The Patron Saint of Czech Skiers

The Krkonoše, or Giant Mountains, are a deep range of steep slopes and dense, impenetrable forest on the northernmost border with Poland. From the 13th century they were inhabited by a sensitive hardy mountain people, who survived the deep blankets of winter snow by singing, telling ghost stories and making strange musical instruments.

They also created a mythical patron, a just ruler who rewarded the good and punished the evil by unleashing snowstorms or fields of flowers. They named him Krakonoš and imagined him as an old man with a long flowing beard, dressed in bright forest green with a hunter's hat. From olden times he was the only authority recognized by sinful folk, and became feared as well as revered. Everyone wanted to be on good terms with the spirit of the Giant Mountains.

To appease their idol, the mountain people would carve his likeness in wood and place figurines around their cottages. By the 19th century his legend had grown to outlandish proportions.

Krakonoš still comes down from the mountains once a year, on the first Saturday in March, during the traditional end-of-winter festival in Harrachov Ski Centre. He arrives amid much pageantry by horse-drawn sleigh, escorted by colourful devils, green jacket flapping in his wake. Though few still believe in his supernatural powers, his popularity, and the pull of this fantastically boisterous carnival, have not declined.

visitors and entertainment. Wander around and take your pick of cellars for your wine-tasting.

Your cellar master will siphon off samples from the large barrels into a tasting jar, something akin in size to a medium size jam jar, which you will be expected to drain each time. The wines offered are a range of of reds and whites and the tasting is usually accompanied by congenial conversation. The cellar master will be pleased to tell you how the family all works together to harvest the grapes for pressing—the cellars are rarely sold, but pass from son to son down the generations.

The best way to reach South Moravia is by car so you can move from village to village, but of course, this method requires one sober driver! Another alternative is to book an inexpensive room at Valtice Château, about 3.5 kilometers (2 miles) from Mikulov or arrange for a coach tour through one of the budding new travel agencies.

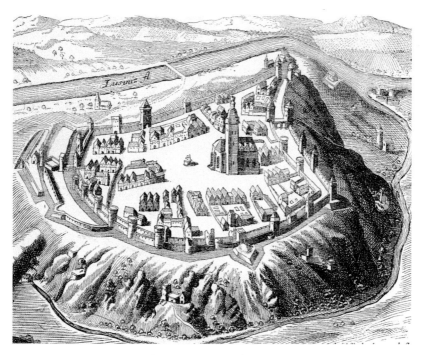

The rocky outcrop of Tabor, surrounded by the Lusinitz and a lake, is the source of many legends

THE SPA TRIANGLE

The image most often brought to mind by the word spa is that of foul-tasting water and members of the geriatric set protecting their blue-rinsed coiffures with thick rubber swimming caps. Although there is an element of truth in this picture, it is only a very small part of the overall image.

To the west of the Czech Republic, the three cities of the Spa Triangle, Karlovy Vary (Karlsbad), Mariánské Lázné (Marienbad) and Františkovy Lázné (František Springs), create a very different picture. Here you will find top-notch clinical facilities nestled comfortably among castles and mansions, set in romantic scenery.

The king of Czech spas is **Karlovy Vary**, 122 kilometres (76 miles) from Prague. Located around a confluence of three rivers, the city rises up on deep forested slopes surrounding the valley. It was at the top of **Stag's Leap** that one of King Charles IV's hunting dogs is said to have chased after a stag, leaping from the hill all the way to Vřídlo Spring. The hound fell into the hot spring and his howling alerted the hunters to the miraculous waters. The statue of a chamois which stands high above the town was placed there by one of Karlovy Vary's early eccentric collectors, Count Lutzow, to commemorate the event.

Czar Peter I first visited Karlovy Vary in 1711, accompanied by his huge entourage. Following his example, royalty, politicians and artists started to visit the area, enhancing its fame and world reputation. Johann Wolfgang Goethe was a frequent visitor, as were Ludwig van Beethoven, Frédéric Chopin and Friedrich Schiller. Other spa devotees were Johannes Brahms, Prince Otto von Bismarck, the Empress Maria Theresa and the more modern hero Soviet astronaut Yuri Gagarin.

Today there are 60-odd thermal springs, rich in dissolved minerals and carbon dioxide. They are particularly good for the treatment of diseases of the digestive system and metabolic disorders. Twelve of the springs boast temperatures ranging from 41° to 73° C (105° to 163° F), the most famous of which is **Vřídlo** which spouts out 2,000 litres per minute from a

Wine tasting

depth of 2,500 metres. The thermal springs reach the surface through bore holes up to 80 metres (262 feet) deep.

The mineral waters are used for drinking cures and baths as well as the extraction of mineral salts. Water taken from the **Mlýnský pramen** (Mill Spring) is bottled and visitors often buy souvenirs made of sinter, a type of clay produced by the spring. The best way to enjoy the water, however, is to sit back in one of the gorgeous gazebos and sip the warm soapy tasting water from a special spigot mug that you will see for sale everywhere.

You will not want to miss a taste from the thirteenth spring, however. That is the nickname of the local aperitif, *becherovka*. It has been produced according to pharmacist Josef Becher's secret recipe of ancient herbs for over 200 years. Bottles of the golden liquor make a tasty souvenir—purely for medicinal purposes of course—for your non-teetotal friends.

It is said that everybody who wanted to be somebody in Europe in the last century had to appear in Karlovy Vary from time to time. It is obvious even now that they came to the spa not only to improve their health by taking the waters and baths, but to meet other people, to entertain and be entertained. The hallmark of European turn-of-the-century social style is evident everywhere, but nowhere more than in the majestic **Grand Hotel Pupp**, a triumph of gloriously opulent architecture.

Nearby **Mariánské Lázné** is considered the pearl of Czech spas. The first experiments with the local waters were conducted during the 16th century when attempts were made to extract edible salt by evaporation. Rumour has it that such experiments continued for two centuries before they were finally abandoned. The small town became a public spa in 1818, and was once a fashionable resort for the noble and the rich.

In 1822, Johann Wolfgang Goethe described it to a friend as 'perfect accommodation, pleasant hosts, good company, pretty girls, music lovers, good evening entertainment, delicious food, new acquaintances with prominent people'. A statue commemorating Goethe's unrequited love for Ulrika von Levetzow, detailed in his *Marienbader Elegie*, lies near the Forest Spring.

You get quite a heady feeling strolling the cobblestones once trodden by the likes of Chopin, Wagner, Ibsen, Freud, Kafka and Kipling. Their visits are honoured by many statues and plaques around town. Furthermore, you can even soak in the same bathtub used by King Edward VII of England and visit his favourite room at the Hotel Kavkaz, a stunning architectural dinosaur.

Tucked up in the fir-clad hills are other magical and mystical statues, surrounded by forest fertility legends. Just behind the Junior Hotel, a romantic old hunting lodge three miles up in a mountaintop eyrie, you will see statues of elves, gnomes and fairies in enchanting wild flower gardens and hiking trails.

The city itself is like a Victorian painting of washed pastel façades against a lush green backdrop. **Skalnik Gardens**, designed and landscaped by Václav Skalnik, lines the entire length of the town with a brilliant profusion of colourful flower beds spilling over its slopes. The crowning glory, however, is the former Maxima Gorkého, now **Kreuzbrunnen Colonnade**, and the **Singing Fountain**, which performs a daily selection of concerts every two hours from 07:00 and ends with an evening show at 22:00. Eighteen metres (fifty-nine feet) across, the hundreds of dancing water jets play to the accompaniment of piped music by Strauss, Rossini, Dvořák, Chopin and more. In the summer months special theatre performances also add charm to the vast garden surrounding the colonnade and the stately spa building **Kasino**.

The cream coloured iron, wood and glass expanse of the colonnade, built in 1889, houses six springs, open for sampling daily from 06:00 to noon and 16:00 to 18:00. Modern taps bring the hot medicinal waters gushing forth at a wave of the hand. Plastic cups can be bought for 2 kčs, or you can rent one of the proper spigots for about 100 kčs.

Café on the Alteweise, Karlovy Vary, c. 1880

In the park below you can see the memorial erected in honour of the US Army troops who liberated the town at the end of World War II. At the bottom of the garden, cross the street to the tiny Ambrose Spring, which is reportedly good for the treatment of anaemia. According to legend, if a young woman serves a man water from this spring from her hands, he will fall hopelessly in love with her. If the man then serves her in the same manner, the love will sparkle eternally and she will remain faithful forever.

Of all the spa towns, Mariánské Lázné boasts the largest selection of springs (more than 140 of them). However, only 39 of these springs are used for curative purposes, which involve drinking and bathing in the gushing spring waters. Each spring is reputed to cure a different ailment, in particular those related to diseases of the kidney, urinary and respiratory tracts. Unfortunately, you must drink 1.5 litres of water per day for a period of 21 days to get the full beneficial effects. The most enjoyably potable water can be found at a small spring just on the outskirts of town where Prague residents arrive with dozens of plastic bottles to haul home their monthly supply.

The springs at Mariánské Lázné, rich in carbon dioxide and mineral salts, can be divided into five healing groups:

- The **Cross** and **Ferdinand Springs** treat gastric, gall bladder, liver, pancreas and metabolic disorders.
- Drinking from the **Forest Spring** heals diseases of the respiratory tract and inhalation of the vapours treats gastrointestinal and urinary tract ailments.
- The **Excelsior Spring** and the **Caroline Spring** are beneficial to urological disorders.
- The **Ambrose Spring** aids anaemia.
- The **Rudolph Spring** treats diseases of the kidneys and urinary tract.

Františkovy Lázné, although the smallest of the three spas, is perhaps the most elegant. This charming park retreat, near the border town of Cheb, owes its existence to a women's rebellion. Early history has recorded settlements at the peat bogs near the village of Slatina in the period between the Bronze and Stone Ages. Even at that time, salts were obtained from the springs and mud from the bogs through evaporation over fire. In the 5th century AD, Slav tribes replaced the Celts, and later came Germanic settlers.

In chronicles dating from 1406, the waters were described as joyous due to their bubbling, sparkling nature. By 1572, the waters were officially analyzed and in 1584 the first spa guest came to stay in Cheb.

The springs so enchanted Queen Anne, wife of Matthias of Vienna, that by 1620 many members of the German royal family came to visit, as well as the Polish King Sigismund. Cheb became wealthy from the business of dispatching the waters all over Europe.

Dr Bernhard Adler, credited with founding the spa in 1793, decided that the spring was not adequately protected. He claimed it would become polluted if the water business continued. To avoid this, he built a pavilion over the spring, thus putting a stranglehold on the profitable income earned by Cheb's womenfolk as water carriers. So it was that just after midnight three platoons of women, led by the wives of a bricklayer, publican and shoemaker, went on the warpath. Armed with domestic implements, flails and axes, they swarmed František Spring and demolished the pavilion, attacked the male workers and Dr Adler, and celebrated with a victory dance.

Though Dr Adler pleaded with the new King of Bohemia, Emperor Leopold II, the springs were returned to the people of Cheb, the women escaped punishment and became the founders of the new spa, which, for many years after, treated only women's diseases.

Created as a sort of fanciful enclave in Empire and classical styles, the spa grew and prospered. Many famous names appear in the visitor's book including the philosophers Fichte and Herder, Marshal Blucher who defeated Napoleon and Empress Marie Louise, whose name is borne by one of the springs. In 1812, Ludwig van

Beethoven composed his *Seventh Symphony in F Major* while a patient at the Sevastopol Sanatorium.

Though the two world wars brought structural damage and a change of clientele, Františkovy Lázné was eventually restored to its original beauty. It is said that life here reflects the world as we would like to see it, presented in its best colours. Perhaps that is why the treatments from the 24 springs of this volcanic area are often so successful.

Indeed, at one time they were considered too successful. The František Spring was once deemed so powerful that young men forbade their girlfriends to drink from it so as not to become mothers too soon. Touching the statue of the little boy, Francis, is also considered to have magical powers and to help in cases of sterility. The **Palliardi Spring**, also called the **Spring of Love** or **Youth**, is reported to have rejuvenating powers and to preserve physical and mental abilities. Whatever the case, young men in Prague still joke about visiting Františkovy Lázné to offer their services to young women visiting the spa for treatment.

For those having no need for extensive treatment, Františkovy Lázné's central spa offers massage therapy and has exercise and swimming facilities. There is also a movie theatre, miniature golf course, tennis courts and a disco. The local museum, the **Městské Muzeum**, is open from Monday to Friday, 08:00–12:00, and in the afternoon every day except Tuesday from 14:00–18:00. An exhibition of photographs, drawings and an assortment of equipment details the history of the spas.

For more information on all the spas contact: Balnea Travel, Pařížska 11, Prague 1. Tel (02) 232 37 67 or fax 232 19 38.

Karlštejn Castle (25 kilometres from Prague), built by Charles IV

Practical Information

Useful Addresses

EMERGENCY TELEPHONE NUMBERS

Airport	36 78 16, 36 78 14
AT&T USA Direct	00 42 000 101
Customs	232 22 70
Emergency Medical Aid	
(English and German)	29 93 81
Police	2121 1111
Prague Information Centre	
Vikářská 37	2101, ext 3368
Prague Information Service	54 44 44
Taxi	20 29 51, 20 39 41
Train Information	26 49 30, 236 44 41

AIRLINE OFFICES

Aeroflot
Pařížská 5, Prague 1.
Tel 232 3333

British Airways
Staroměstské nám 10, Prague 1.
Tel 232 90 20

Air France
Václavské nám 10, Prague 1.
Tel 26 01 55

ČSA
Revoluční 1, Prague 1 (opposite Kotva).

International flights	Tel 231 25 95, 235 27 85
Domestic flights	Tel 232 20 06
Information Office	Tel 231 73 95
Airport Information	Tel 36 78 14, 36 77 60

Air India
Václavské nám 15, Prague 1.
Tel 22 38 54

Alitalia
Revoluční 5, Prague 1.
Tel 231 05 35

Delta
Narodní 32, Prague 1.
Tel 232 47 72 06

Austrian Airlines
Pařížská 1, Prague 1.
Tel 232 45 00, 232 64 69

Finnair
Španělská 2, Prague 2.
Tel 22 30 12, 22 64 89

KLM
Václavské nám 37, Prague 1.
Tel 26 43 62, 26 43 69

Kuwait Airways
Pařížská 23, Prague 1.
Tel 231 10 89, 231 14 72

Lufthansa
Pařížská 28, Prague 1. Tel 248 10 94

SAS Scandinavian Airlines
Štěpánská 61, Prague 1.
Tel 22 81 41

Swissair
Pařížská 11, Prague 1.
Tel 232 66 05, 232 47 07

BANKS
Čekobanka Chequepoint
Čeletná 18, Prague 1
08:00–21:00

Komerční banka
Na příkopě 28, Prague 1.
Mon–Fri 08:00–18:30

Obchodní banka
Na příkopě 14, Prague 1.
Mon–Fri 07:30–12:00

Státní banka československá
Václavské nám 42, Prague 1.
Mon–Fri 08:30–13:00

Živnostenská banka
Na příkopě 20, Prague 1.
Mon–Fri 08:00–17:00, Sat 08:00–12:00

■ **EXCHANGE OFFICES**
Čedok Travel Agency
Na příkopě 18, Prague 1.
Mon–Fri 08:15–18:00

Kotva Department Store
Náměstí Republiky 8, Prague 1.
Mon–Fri 10:00–18:00, Sat 08:00–15:00

There are also exchange offices at:
Ruzyně Airport, Main Railway Station
(Hlavní nádraží), the Jalta Hotel and the
Diplomat Hotel.

■ **CHEQUEPOINT EXCHANGE OFFICES**
Prague Castle, Third Courtyard
09:00–18:00
Staroměstské nám 27 (Old Town Square)
07:30–21:00
Václavské nám 1 (Wenceslas Square)
07:30–21:00

EMBASSIES
Austria
Viktora Huga 10, Prague 5. Tel 54 65 57

Belgium
Valdštejnská 6, Prague 1. Tel 53 40 51

Bulgaria
Krakovská 6, Prague 1. Tel 26 43 10

Canada
Mickiewiczova 6, Prague 6.
Tel 312 02 51

CIS
Pod kaštany 1, Prague 6. Tel 38 19 40

Postal Work

Nine letters in my hand, I crossed Jindřišská Street and turned towards Prague's main Post Office. My fingers separated three distinct piles of letters that I had written in the last week: three to the United States, three to Germany and three withinin Czechoslovakia. With constantly changing prices, I wanted to be sure that each destination received the appropriate postage.

Thirty-odd booths lined the far wall of the Post Office. Off in a corner by itself stood a small glass cabin lined with stamps. Two whole sides of the 5 x 6 cabin were layered in postal stamps, of all values, shapes and sizes. In between sat a nondescript man, much like an elderly guard at a Museum of Natural History—the type one is accustomed to when purchasing stamps. His stool was too high so he was slouching a bit as I approached him with my three orderly piles.

It took fifteen minutes for me to get my nine letters stamped, but I came away with postal pieces of art so touching I regretted disposing of them in the mail box. For each of the three countries, my Bohemian postal craftsman carefully selected a series of stamps. Each letter received a unique stamp within the series, to protect its individuality, while each national triplet had its own defining motif.

He plucked each stamp delicately from the wall with his tweezers and placed them neatly on the appropriate envelopes. For Germany he chose the industrial motif, a clear cultural association: shining turbines and grinding gears in the art nouveau style for this industrial neighbor. For America the stamp artist selected a series on the Prague castle depicting the various treasures within its walls. King Poděbrady's crown, Charles IV's flasks, and artifacts of this nation's historical wealth stood in contrast to its younger sibling across the sea. Finally, for Czechoslovakia, modes of transportation: automobiles, planes and trains. I thought of the gold-painted East German Trabant sitting atop four huge legs in the Old Town Square for months following the 1989 revolution. Its license plate read in Czech: 'Where are we going?'

The amazing aspect of all this was the extreme care this outwardly emotionless man took in his stamps. For fifteen minutes this was an art, an all-important process, regardless of the line behind me that was winding out the door.

Fred Abrahams, from Yazzyk Magazine Issue One, 1992

Fred Abrahams is an American working for the Prague office of the human rights organization Helsinki Citizen's Assembly.

Cuba
Sibiřské nám 1, Prague 6. Tel 34 13 41

Denmark
U Havlíčkových sadů 1, Prague 2.
Tel 25 47 15

France
Velkopřevorské nám 2, Prague 1.
Tel 53 30 42

Germany
Vlašská 19, Prague 1. Tel 53 23 51

Hungary
Mičurinova 1, Prague 6. Tel 36 50 41

Italy
Nerudova 20, Prague 1. Tel 53 06 66

Netherlands
Maltézské nám, Prague 1. Tel 53 13 78

Poland
Valdštejnská 8, Prague 1. Tel 53 69 51

Romania
Nerudova 5, Prague 1. Tel 53 30 59

Spain
Pevnostní 9, Prague 6. Tel 32 71 24

Sweden
Úvoz 13, Prague 1. Tel 53 33 44

Switzerland
Pevnostní 7, Prague 6. Tel 32 83 19

United Kingdom
Thunovská 14, Prague 1.
Tel 53 33 47, 53 33 70

United States of America
Tžišté 15, Prague 1. Tel 53 66 41

Yugoslavia
Můstecka 15, Prague 1.
Tel 53 14 43

ENTERTAINMENT
■ CINEMAS
Alfa
Václavské nám 28, Prague 1.
Tel 22 07 24

Blanik
Václavské nám 56, Prague 1.
Tel 235 21 62

Hvezda
Václavské nám 38, Prague 1.
Tel 22 91 87

Illusion
Vinohradská 48, Prague. Tel 25 02 60

Květen
Vinohradská 40, Prague. Tel 25 33 41

Lucerna
Vodičkova 36, Prague. Tel 235 26 48

Paříž
Václavské nám 22, Prague 1.
Tel 235 76 97

Pasá
Václavské nám 5, Prague 1.
Tel 235 50 40

THE SUBURBS
Aero
Biskupova 31, Prague. Tel 89 36 01

Eden
U Slávie 1, Prague. Tel 74 70 39

Kosmos
Sídliště Novadvorská. Tel 472 37 30

■ JAZZ CLUBS
Agharta Jazz Centre
Krakovská 5, Prague 1. Tel 22 45 58.
Open Mon to Fri from 10:00–24:00, Sat
and Sun from 17:00–24:00.

Jazz Art Club
Vinohradská 40, Prague 2. Tel 25 76 54.
Open Tue to Sun from 20:00–02:00. Per-
formances from 21:30.

Jazz Club Luxor
American Music Club, Václavské nám 41,
Prague 1. Open daily 20:00–24:00.

Press Jazz Club
Pařížská 9, Prague 1. Tel 22 47 23. Jazz
concerts orientated at swing and main-
stream held every Thursday 21:00–24:00.

Reduta
Národní 20, Prague 1. Tel 20 38 25
Music begins at 21:30, ticket office
opens at 21:00.

Supraclub–Night Jazz Club
Opletalova 5, Prague 1. Concerts held on
Fri, Sat and Sun 21:00–03:00. Bar
open during performances.

■ ROCK
Barclub/Reggae Sound System
Hybernská 10, Prague 1. Daily 22:00–
05:00. Afro/reggae on Mon, Wed–Sun.
Rockin' 60s on Tues.

Belmondo Revival Club
Slavíčkova 22, Prague 3. Open daily
19:00–01:00. Converted theatre with
huge dance floor and moderately priced
drinks.

Classic Club
Pařížská 4, Prague 1. Daily 12:00–03:00.
Large dance floor with music varying
from LA-style to Cat Stevens and Cher.

Mamma Club
Elišky Krásnohorské 7, Prague 1.
Tel 232 6912. Open Tues–Sun 10:00–
20:00. Occasionally has DJ or live music,
hot and smoky room downstairs.

New D Club
Vinohradská 38, Prague 2. Daily 21:00–
02:00. Mon folk; Tues country; Wed and
Sat reggae; Thu rock; Fri dance; Sun jazz.

Rock Café
Národní 20, Prague 1. Tel 20 66 56.
Open Mon to Sat 10:00–18:00. Consist-
ently good live rock.

Újezd Club
Újezd 18, Prague 1. Open Fri and Sat
18:00–06:00, Wed and Sun 20:00–05:00.

ART EXHIBITIONS AND
COMMERCIAL GALLERIES
Artoteka
Dolanského 1754, Prague 4.
Tel 791 87 59
Open Mon 13:00–19:00, Tues 09:00–
18:00, Wed 12:00–18:00

Atrium
Čajkovského 12, Prague 3. Tel 27 40 80
Open Tues to Sun 14:00–17:00

Benediktská Galerie
Benediktská 12, Prague 1.
Open Mon to Sat 10:00–17:00

Bistro-Galerie Olin
Kafkova 33, Prague 6.
Open Mon to Fri, 12:00–21:00

Central Czech Graphics Gallery
(Galerie GGG Centrum české grafity)
Husova 10, Prague 1.
Open Tues and Fri 11:00–18:00, Sat
10:00–20:00

Chodovská Vodní Tvrz
Ledvinova 9, Prague 4.
Open Tues to Fri 13:00–19:00, Sat and
Sun 10:00–13:00, 14:00–18:00

Galerie Albaros
Národní, Prague 1.
Open daily 09:30–18:00

Galerie Behemot
Elišky Krásnohorské 6, Prague 1.
Open daily 10:00–19:00

Galerie Bohm
Anglická 1, Prague 2.
Open Tues to Fri 14:00–18:00, Sat and
Sun 10:00–15:00

Galerie Bratří Čapků
Jugoslávská 20, Prague 2.
Open daily 10:00–13:00, 14:00–18:00

Galerie Centrum
ul 28 října 6, Prague 1.
Open Mon to Fri 10:00–18:00, Sat
09:00–12:00

Galerie D
Matoušova 9, Prague 5.
Open daily 10:00–13:00, 14:00–18:00
Carpets and cloth

Galerie Karolina
Železná 6, Prague 1.
Open Mon to Fri 10:00–18:00, Sat
11:00–12:00

Galerie Letná
Horáčková 22, Prague 7.
Open Mon to Fri 10:00–18:00,
Sat 10:00–13:00

Galerie Luka
Mukařovského 1985, Prague 5.
Open Mon to Sat 14:00–19:00

Window in the Museum of Decorative Arts designed by architect Josef Schulz

Galerie Malý Platýz
nádvoří Platýz, Národní 37, Prague 1.
Open Mon to Fri 10:00–18:00,
Sat 09:00–12:00

Galerie Mladá fronta
Spálená 53, Prague 1. Tel 29 45 08
Open daily

Galerie Modrý Pavilon
Štúrsova 1282, Prague 4.
Open Tues to Sun 10:00–18:00

Galerie na Můstku
28 října 16, Prague 1.
Open Mon to Fri 10:00–18:00,
Sat 09:00–12:00

Galerie Platýz
Národní 37, Prague 1.
Open Mon to Fri 10:00–18:00,
Sat 10:00–13:00

Galerie R
Táborská 65, Prague 4.
Open Tues to Sat 10:00–18:00

Galerie Svazu Českých Fotografů
Kamzíková 8, Prague 1.
Open daily 12:00–18:00

Galerie Vavrys
Rytířská 11, Prague 1.
Open daily 10:00–19:00

House at the Stone Bell (Dům u kamenného zvonu)
Staroměstské nám 13, Prague 1.

Mánes
Masarykovo nábř 250, Prague 1.
Open daily 10:00–18:00

Municipal Gallery of Prague
(Galerie H M Prahy)
Staroměstské nám 1, Staroměstská radnice, Prague 1. Tel 84 51 33

Prague Castle (Prazký hrad)
Open daily 09:00–17:00
Permanent exhibition: paintings of the 16th–18th centuries; treasures; crafts of the 9th–19th centuries.

Museums, including Art Collections

Central Bohemian Museum
(Středočeské muzeum)
Roztoky u Prahy. Tel 39 61 80

Comenius Pedagogical Museum
(Pedagogické muzeum J A Komenskéko)
Valdštejnské nám, Prague 1.
Open Tues to Sun 10:00–12:00,
13:00–17:00

Jewish Museum (Židovské muzeum)
Maiselova 10, Prague 1. Tel 23 10 718

Loreta
Loretánské nám 7, Prague 1.
Tel 53 62 28
Open daily 09:00–12:00, 13:00–17:00

Memorial of National Literature
(Památník národního písemnictví)
Strahov Monastary Courtyard 1,
off Pohořelec nám, Prague 1.
Tel 53 62 28. Open daily 09:30–17:00

Military Museum (Vojenské muzeum)
Exhibition of the Resistance and Czechoslovak Army
U Památníku 2, Prague 3. Tel 27 29 65
Open Tuesday to Sunday, 09:30–16:30

Museum of African, Asian and American Culture (Náprstkovo muzeum)
Betlémské nám 1, Prague 1. Tel 22 76 91
Permanent exhibits: Ancient Egyptian amulets, epigraphics on Islamic arms, Indian cultures of Northern and Southern America, cultures of Australian and Pacific Islands.

Museum of Alois Jirásek and Mikuláš Aleš
(Muzeum Aloise Jirásek a Mikuláš Aleš)
Letohradek Hvezda, Prague 6.
Tel 36 79 38

Museum of Decorative Art
(Umćleckoprůmyslové muzeum v Praze)
17 Listopadu 2, Prague 1. Tel 232 0017
Open Tues to Sun 10:00–18:00

Museum of the Police
(Muzeum policie MV CR)
Ke Karlovu, Prague 1. Tel 29 89 40
Open daily 10:00–17:00

National Gallery of Prague
(Národní galerie v Praze)
The National Gallery maintains eight separate galleries throughout Prague, which are as follows:

Goltz-Kinsky Palace (Palác Kinských)
Staroměstské nám 12, Prague 1.
Tel 23 15 35

Municipal Library (Městská knihovna)
Mariánské nám, Prague 1.

Prague Castle Riding School
(Jízdarna Pražkého hradu)
U Prašného mostu 55, Prague 1.
Tel 21 01
Czech art 1908–1968

St George's Convent
(Klášter sv Jiří na Pražkém hradé)
Jirske nám 33, Prague 1.

St Agnes Convent
(Klášter sv Anežky České)
U milosrdných 17, Prague 1.
Viennese Gothic art—sculptures, paintings on glass and architectural statues from Vienna's St Stephen's Cathedral.

Sternberg Palace (Šternberský palác)
Hradcánské nám 15, Prague 1.
Tel 352 44 13
Open Tues to Sun 10:00–18:00

Wallenstein Riding School
(Valdštejnská jízdarna)
Klarov, Malostranská metro station,
Prague 1.

Zbraslav Château (Zámek Zbraslav)
Prague 5.
Czech sculptures displayed for the blind.

National Museum
(Národní Muzeum v Praze)
Václavské nám 68, Prague 1.
Tel 269 45 17
Open Wed to Sun 09:00–17:00,
Mon and Fri to 16:00

National Museum at Lobkovic Palace
(Národní Muzeum, Lobkovický palác)
Praském hradě, Prague 1. Tel 53 73 06
Tues to Sun 09:00–17:00

National Museum of Technology
(Národní technické muzeum)
Kostelní 42, Prague 7. Tel 373 66 51

National Science Museum
(Šternberkovo Přírovědné Muzeum)
Ovčarská 418, Prague 10. Tel 77 44 57

Old Jewish Cemetery
(Starý Židovský hřbitov)
17 Listopadu 2, Prague 1.

Prague Municipal Museum
(Muzeum hlavního města Prahy)
Švermovy sady 1554, Prague 1.
Tel 236 24 50

PETROL STATIONS
All stations listed are open 24 hours:
Olšanka, Prague 3. Tel 27 88 15
Újezd (Autobahn), Prague 4.
Tel 75 91 05
Plzeňská, Prague 5. Tel 52 04 70
Českobrodská, Prague 9. Tel 82 50 53
Prosecká, Prague 9. Tel 88 92 84

SHOPPING
Department Stores in the centre of
Prague)
Bílá Labut
Na poříčí 23, Nové město, Prague 1.
Tel 232 06 22

(above and right) *Museum of Decorative Arts*

Druzba
Václavské nám 21, Nové město,
Prague 1. Tel 26 38 42

Kotva
Náměstí Republiky 8, Nové město,
Prague 1. Tel 235 00 01

Maj
Národní 26, Nové město, Prague 1.
Tel 26 23 41

■ ANTIQUES
Čeletná 31, Staré město, Prague 1.
Tel 232 29 29
Antiques and coins

Melantrichova 9, Staré město, Prague 1.
Tel 26 21 86

■ **BOHEMIAN CRYSTAL**
Bohemia
Staroměstské nám 6, Prague 1.
Tel 232 77 71
Mon to Fri 10:00–18:00, Sat 09:00–13:00

■ **BOHEMIA-MOSER**
Na příkopě 12, Nové město, Prague 1.
Tel 22 18 51
Mon to Fri 08:30–19:00, Sat 09:00–13:00
Payment is possible in Czech crowns,
foreign currency and credit cards.

Mikulandská 7, Nové město, Prague 1.
Tel 29 86 09

Milady Horákové 27, Holešovice,
Prague 7. Tel 37 46 50

Mostecká 7, Malá strana, Prague 1.
Tel 53 12 98

Na můstku 5, Staré město, Prague 1.
Tel 26 00 91

Národní 22, Nové město, Prague 1.
Tel 29 41 70

Národní 24, Nové město, Prague 1.
Tel 26 20 33

Nerudova 46, Malá strana, Prague 1.
Tel 53 41 61

Uhelný trh 6, Staré město, Prague 1.
Tel 22 55 36

Vinohradská 45, Vinohrady, Prague 2.
Tel 25 47 81

Crystalex
Malé nám 6, Prague 1. Tel 26 36 94
Mon to Fri 08:30–18:00, Sat 09:00–13:00

Diamant
Václavské nám 3, Prague 1. Tel 22 90 41
Mon to Fri 08:30–18:00, Sat 08:30–13:00

Krystal
Václavské nám 30, Prague 1.
Tel 26 33 84
Mon to Fri 08:30–18:00, Sat 09:00–13:00

Lux
Na příkopě 14, Nové město, Prague 1.
Tel 22 06 19
Mon to Fri 10:00–18:00
Crystal chandeliers and miniature animal
figurines.

■ **FOLK ART**
Česká jizba
Karlova 12, Staré město, Prague 1.
Tel 26 57 73

CASINOS

Decadent, bourgeois, capitalistic, evil. What better than words of condemnation to make a society crave the forbidden? Despite 48 years of absolute prohibition under absolute Communist rule, gambling has returned with a vengeance.

Casino owners in particular have capitalized on the new-found freedom. Casinos Austria, Čedok's joint venture partner into the world of vice is undoubtedly the most prestigious of the new casino owners. Their overall revenue for 1991 was over US$8 million and the figures for 1992 are forecast to be even higher.

Though the Czechoslovak casinos are not on the same opulent par as those of Monte Carlo, they do fill a gap in the marketplace, that of evening entertainment. Unfortunately, it is the one glaring hole in the tourist trade market yet to be plugged.

All Prague's casinos have a dress code level of casual chic. In other words, no jeans, T-shirts and sneakers. The idea is actually to help teach a little refinement, according to Lubos Jelínek, a representative for Novomatic. Their casino has a complete wardrobe from which people can borrow clothes to change into, though on many evenings supplies run out very early.

Novomatic owns **The Admiral Casino** at the Palace of Culture and draws huge crowds of mostly younger locals and less formal tourists. Vintage Madonna drones over the PA system and the minimum bet on American roulette and black jack is 20 kčs (about US$0.66). Only sparkling wine by the bottle in on sale at the revamped bar, and the atmosphere is enhanced by the musical chatter of 40 slot machines.

The tiny **Hotel Forum Casino** is usually packed with a much more upscale crowd of potential highrollers—a few Japanese businessmen sur-

Krašna jizba
Národní 36, Nové město, Prague 1.
Tel 2366535

Slovénska jizba
Václavské nám 40, Nové město, Prague 1. Tel 235 29 67

■ JEWELLERS'
Národní 25, Nové město, Prague 1.
Tel 26 20 29

Na příkopě 12, Nové město, Prague 1.
Tel 22 06 19

rounded by well-dressed Middle Easterners and a gaggle of German house-wives on a weekend coach tour. The atmosphere is quieter, the drinks more expensive and games are played in US dollars. As in all the hotel casinos, minimum bets are US$2 for American roulette and US$5 for black jack; however, there are no slot machines. Since the crowd is mostly hotel guests with the occasional carefully escorted local female, it is perfectly comfortable to wander in and while away a few hours and a few dollars.

The **Ambassador Hotel Casino** has a good continental feel once you push your way through the clutch of pimps, prostitutes and black market money changers blocking the Wenceslas Square entrance. The spacious open balcony with its splash of plants and crystal chandeliers overlooks a decent restaurant and a live combo band lends a certain tropical flavor. The **Palace Hotel Casino** is also on a balcony above the restaurant. Unlike the Ambassador, the space is closed in giving it a clubby feel.

The most exclusive, and smallest, of the Prague casinos is the **Diplomatic Club** tucked along Karlova Street near the Charles Bridge. Though actually intended for diplomats and visiting dignitaries, a well-dressed client can enter without problems. The cuisine is one of Prague's best and private rooms can be booked for parties from four to twenty people.

There is also a slot machine-only casino in the passageway next to the Ambassador Hotel. This draws a rather colourful *mélange* of locals and tourists and sees action from 11:00 to well past midnight.

Gambling hours for Prague casinos:
Diplomatic Club: 20:00–04:00
Hotel Ambassador: 16:00–04:00
Hotel Forum: 18:00–04:00
Palace Hotel : 19:30–04:00
The Admiral: 18:00–06:00

Václavské nám 28, Nové město, Prague 1. Tel 26 11 98

Václavské nám 53, Nové město, Prague 1. Tel 22 83 34

ul 28 října 15, Staré město, Prague 1. Tel 26 71 65

■ MUSIC
Jungmannova 30, Prague 1. Tel 22 30 06
Sheet music

Jungmannovo nám 17, Prague 1. Tel 236 13 76
Musical instruments

Na příkopě 24, Prague 1. Tel 22 11 90
Antique sheet music

■ SOUVENIRS
Václavské nám 47, Staré město, Prague 1.
Tel 26 57 87

Staroměstské nám 6, Staré město, Prague 1. Tel 231 81 19

Uluv
Národní 36, Prague 1. Tel 26 10 51

Uva
Na příkopě 25, Staré město, Prague 1.
Tel 26 28 79

■ TOYS AND DOLLS
Baby Souvenirs
Čeletná 1, Staré město, Prague 1.
Tel 231 17 24

Malé nám 10, Staré město, Prague 1.
Tel 26 28 35

Cajka (Russian Shop)
Železná 24, Prague 1. Tel 22 64 36
Mon to Fri 09:00–18:00, Sat 09:00–13:00

Darky Gifts outlets:
corner of Rytiřská and Můstek, Prague 1.
Tel 269 48 39
Mon to Fri 09:00–19:00, Sat 09:00–13:00
Staroměstké nám 6, Prague 1.
Tel 231 77 71
Mon to Fri 09:00–19:00, Sat 09:00–13:00
Mostecká 8, Prague 1. Tel 53 24 05

Mon to Fri 08:30–12:00, 14:00–18:00,
Sat 09:00–13:00

Umelecka Remesla (Arts and Crafts)
Na můstku 2, Prague 1. Tel 22 34 07
Mon to Fri 08:30–18:00, Sat 08:30–18:30

Zadruha
Železná 7, Prague 1. Tel 236 97 34
Mon to Fri 09:00–18:00, Sat 09:00–13:00

SPORTS FACILITIES
■ INDOOR POOLS
House of Physical Culture
(Dům kultury téla)
Nábřeží kpt Jaroše, Prague 1.
Tel 53 65 20

Park of Culture and Recreation
Stromovka Park, Prague 7. Tel 37 54 04

Plavecký stadión (Swimming Stadium)
Podolská, Prague 4. Tel 42 73 84

Sports club, Slavia Praha
Vladivostocká, Prague 10. Tel 73 85 52

■ SAUNA BATHS
House of Physical Culture
Nábřeží kpt Jaroše, Prague 1.
Tel 53 66 11

Plavecký stadión (Swimming Stadium)
Podolská, Prague 4. Tel 43 91 52

Zluté lázné (Lido on the Vltava)
Podolské nábřeží, Prague 4. Tel 43 14 25

Shoe vendor near Old Town Square, c. 1940

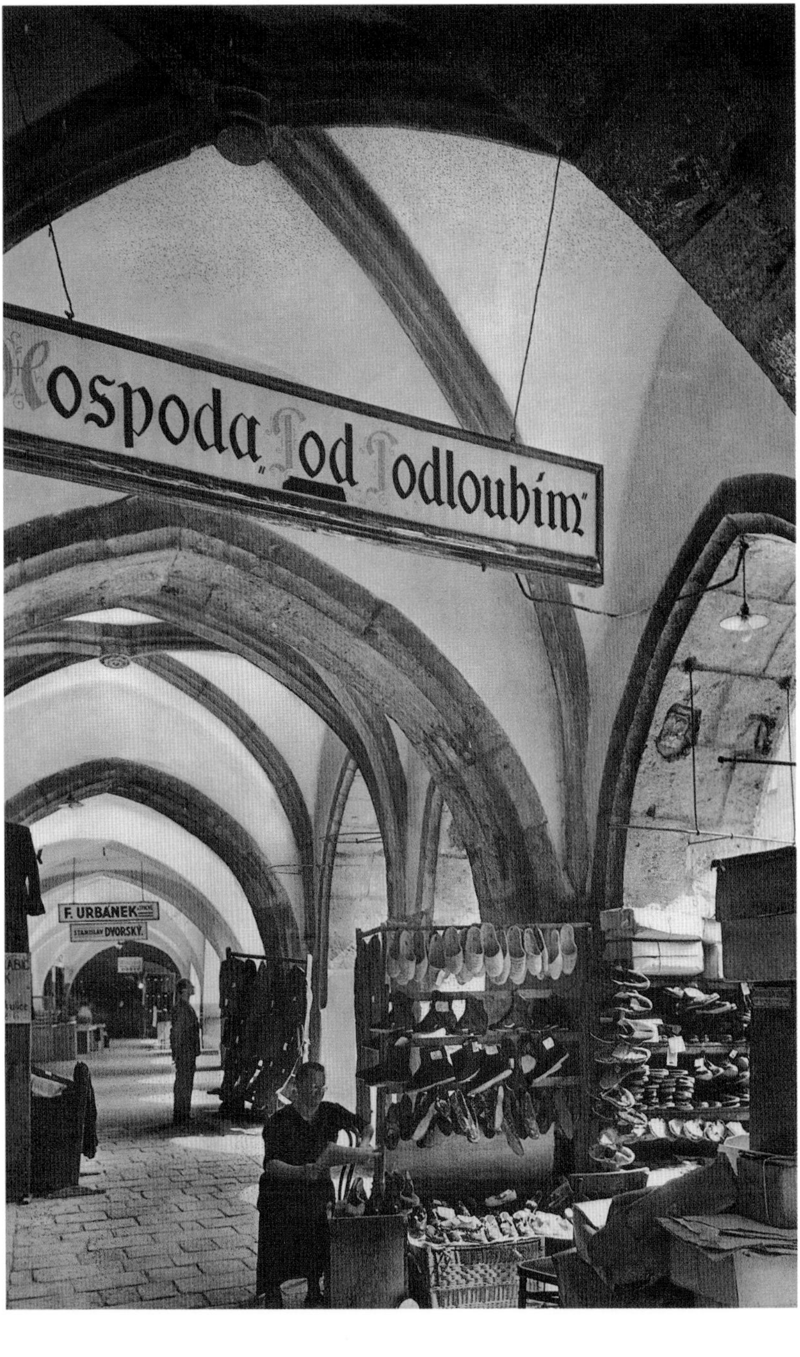
Hospoda „Pod Podloubím"
F. URBÁNEK
STANISLAV DVORSKÝ

Hotels

Though Prague is quickly catching up with the West in terms of hotels the demand for rooms will far exceed the supply for some time to come. It is highly recommended that you book in advance and obtain a written confirmation of your reservation.

■ **FIRST CLASS**

Atrium
Pobřežní 1, Prague 8. Tel 284 11 11
Opened in 1991 with all the modern conveniences one could want. Superb health and fitness facilities. Good food and wine. Excellent beauty shop.

Diplomat
Evropská 1, 160 00 Prague 6.
Tel 331 41 11, fax 34 17 31
Opened 1990. Slightly outside the city centre but very good convention facilities and easy access to metro.

Forum
Kongresová, Prague 4. Tel 419 01 11
Part of the Forum group with all the conveniences. Located adjacent to the Palace of Culture and though outside the city centre is convenient to metro. Very nice fitness centre, good restaurants, casino.

Hotel Palace Praha
Panská 12, Prague 1. Tel 236 00 08
A 100-year-old establishment that was restored and reopened in 1989 with every modern convenience. Centrally located. Good food and piano bar.

Intercontinental
Nám Curieových 5, Prague 1, Staré město. Tel 52 89 9

One of Prague's first top quality hotels right in the middle of Josefov and within blocks of Old Town Square

■ **MODERATE**

Ambassador
Václavské nám 5, Prague 1. Tel 22 13 51
Right in the middle of Wenceslas Square with easy access to everything. Busy, noisy, not as modern as the Hotel Palace, but certainly central.

Esplanade
Washingtonova 19, Prague 1.
Tel 22 25 52
Just off Wenceslas Square. Beautiful old hotel with fine Art Nouveau interior. Rooms are bit small.

Paříž
U Obecního domu 1, Prague 1.
Tel 236 08 20
Popular older hotel not far from Old Town Square.

U tří pštrosů (At the Three Ostriches)
Dražického nám 12, Prague 1.
Tel 53 61 51
Beautiful little hotel nestled at the bottom of Charles Bridge. Arguably the best location in town. Fine restaurant which has been known to be a popular spot

with Václav Havel and friends. Rooms are a little disappointing however.

■ BUDGET

Up-to-date information on youth hostels and camping grounds can be obtained from the International Youth Hostel Association and Pragotour, U Obecního domu 2 (near the Powder Tower).

Restaurants

Dining in Prague used to be a question of luck and a matter of how you wanted your pork and dumplings served. Those days are long past, but so are the days when it was really cheap. Prague now has restaurants to cater to almost every taste with new ones opening almost weekly. Check at your hotel reception and see if they have a copy of *Prague: the heart of Europe*, which will give an updated listing each month. Other than that you can just wander and hope to stumble across some of the best restaurants imaginable. The problem is that most of the time you will need a reservation. You should have a general idea of the cost of a meal before it arrives and then check the bill carefully. Unfortunately Prague is quickly developing a reputation for slightly disreputable waiters. See the vocabulary section (page 187) for food words in case no English menu is available.

Antik Café

Provaznická 1, Prague 1. Tel 26 29 56
A pretty little restaurant just off Wenceslas Square. Hand-painted beamed ceilings, good food and wine.

Crazy Daisy

Vodičkova 9, Prague 1. Tel 23 50 021
Along from New Town Hall, this eatery has the ambience of an American grill and offers medium-priced Czech dishes.

David

Tržiště 21, Prague 1. Tel 53 93 25
A short walk from the American Embassy and catering to the diplomatic and business crowd. Elegant, stylish and expensive.

Nebozízek

Petřínské sady 411, Prague 1.
Tel 53 79 05
Located halfway up Petrín Hill, so take the funicular and enjoy the view. You will also enjoy the food which includes Czech specialities, seafood and some Chinese.

U Červeného Kola (The Red Wheel)

Anežská 2, Prague 1. Tel 231 89 41
Fabulous (international) food in an intimate, romantic surrounding.

Peklo

Strahovské nádvoří 1/130, Prague 1.
Tel 53 02 15

One of the newest additions to the dining scene, this restaurant is located inside the Strahov monastery, one of Prague's oldest buildings. With a dining room upstairs and a disco below, it has become one of the city's trendiest hangouts.

Pod Křídlem
Národní 10, Prague 1. Enter from Voršilská. Tel 21 45 17 41
This white-painted restaurant is just the place to enjoy authentic Czech cuisine without the usual smoky atmosphere.

U Kalicha (At the Chalice)
Na bojišti 12–14 , Prague 2. Tel 29 07 01
A tourist spot for sure, but the former watering hole of Jaroslav Hašek's Good Soldier Švejk is worth a visit.

U Malířů (The Painter's)
Maltézské nám 11. Tel 53 18 83
Walk in this one just for a look—it is one of the most beautiful restaurants in Europe, and priced accordingly.

U Mecenáše (Maecenas')
Malostranské nám 10. Tel 53 38 81
The author's personal favourite! A tiny and beautiful Gothic restaurant with superb food and wine. Prices may have changed drastically since privitization but a dish of caviar is worth the splurge.

U Piaristú
Panská 1, Prague 1. Tel 22 06 03
This used to be a favourite with locals but prices have thinned the non-tourist crowd. Good food, good wine, reasonable prices for city centre.

U Sedmi Andělů (The Seven Angels)
Jilská 20, Prague 1. Tel 26 63 55
An old Prague favourite with good Czech specialities. Near Old Town Square.

U Sixtů
Čeletná 2, Prague 1. Tel 236 79 80
Excellent cuisine in the historic cellars beneath Old Town Square.

U Zátiší (Still Life)
Liliová 1, Betlémské nám. Tel 26 51 07
Not fancy or pretentious, just good local food.

Valdštejnská Hospoda (Waldstein Inn)
Tomášská 16, Prague 1. Tel 53 61 95
A real beauty by Waldstein Gardens. Good food and wine at reasonable prices.

Vinarna Certovka
Luického 1, semináře 24/100, Prague 1.
No telephone
A new little canal-side restaurant that oozes charm if it is warm enough to eat outdoors. It is down a narrow passageway so look out for the sign.

Statue of Handel on the Concert Hall atrium, Rudolfinum

Struggle for Self-Fulfilment

15 August. The time which has just gone by and in which I haven't written a word has been so important for me because I have stopped being ashamed of my body in the swimming pools in Prague, Königssaal and Czernoschitz. How late I make up for my education now, at the age of twenty-eight, a delayed start they would call it at the race track. And the harm of such a misfortune consists, perhaps, not in the fact that one does not win; this is indeed only the still visible, clear, healthy kernel of the misfortune, progressively dissolving and losing its boundaries, that drives one into the interior of the circle, when after all the circle should be run around. Aside from that I have also observed a great many other things in myself during this period which was to some extent also happy, and will try to write it down in the next few days.

20 August. I have the unhappy belief that I haven't the time for the least bit of good work, for I really don't have time for a story, time to expand myself in every direction in the world, as I should have to do. But then I once more believe that my trip will turn out better, that I shall comprehend better if I am relaxed by a little writing, and so try it again.

The Diaries of Franz Kafka, *edited by Max Brod, 1910–23*

Franz Kafka, born in Prague into a Jewish-Czech merchant family in 1883, spent much of his life struggling between the need to earn a living and the consuming need to write. All his books were written in German.

Vocabulary

■ **PRONUNCIATION**

č ch
ch kh
ř rzh
š sh
ž zh
ě ye

■ **COMMON EXPRESSIONS**

yes	ano
no	ne
hello	ahoj
goodbye	nashledanou
good day	dobrý den
Where is the . . .?	Kde je . . .?
excuse me/please	promiňte/prosím
thank you/thanks	děkuji/DK
Do you speak English?	Mluvíte anglicky?
How much is it?	Kolik?
I can't speak Czech.	Nemluvím česky.
more/less/enough	vic/min/dost

■ **NUMBERS**

one/two	jeden/dva
three/four	tři/čtyři
five/six	pět/šest
seven/eight	sedm/osm
nine/ten	devět/deset

■ **AT THE RESTAURANT**

Could we have a table?	Mate prosím volny stul?
The bill, please.	Zaplatím.
I'd like . . .	Prosím . . .
breakfast	snídaně
lunch	oběd
dinner	večeře
vegetarian food	bezmasa jidla

apple	jablko
beef	hovězí maso
beer	pivo
bread	chléb
butter	máslo
cheese	sýr
chicken	kuře
coffee	káva
dumplings	knedlíky
egg	vejce
fish	ryby
french fries	hranolky
fruit	ovoce
ham	šunka
ice-cream	zmrzlinu
jam	dzem
juice	dzus
lemon	citron
meat	maso
milk	mléko
mineral water	minerálku
noodles	nudle
omlette	omeleta
orange	pomeranč
pasta	těstoviny
potatoes	brambory
potato pancake	bramborák
pork	rizek/vepřové maso
rice	rýže
salad	salát
salami	salám
sausage	párek
soup	polévka
sugar	cukr
tea	čaj
vegetables	zelenina
wine	víno

Recommended Reading

Chamberlain, Lesley, *The Food and Cooking of Eastern Europe* (Penguin, London, 1989). This book will whet your appetite and encourage you to walk the streets of Prague in search of good restaurants. Chamberlain ably demonstrates that the food of Eastern European countries goes far beyond goulash and beetroot soup. Recipes are interspersed with quotations, local customs and legends pertaining to the food.

Chatwin, Bruce, *Utz* (Pan Books, London, 1989). A meticulous story of an obsessive collector of porcelain figurines. German-Jew Kasper Utz and his priceless Meissen figures survive Nazi Germany only to become trapped in Communist Czechoslovakia. A tale of the psychology of the compulsive collector told against the back drop of Post-War Prague.

Drakulić, Slavenka, *How We Survived Communism and Even Laughed* (Hutchinson, London, 1992). This is an icebreaker of a book, the first ever critique of Communism from a feminist point of view, written by someone who really does know how women lived in pre-revolutionary Eastern Europe.

Garton Ash, Timothy, *The People: the Revolution of 89* (Granta Books, London, 1990). A popular eye-witness account of the events that changed the face of Europe, written by an informed political observer.

Garton Ash, Timothy, *The Uses of Adversity* (Granta Books, London, 1991). 'His collection of brilliant articles, which not only describe but participate in the cur rent metamorphosis of the Eastern European countries, shows that a British writer can still take the world for scope.' Clive James

Glenny, Misha, *The Rebirth of History, Eastern Europe in the Age of Democracy* (Penguin, London, 1993). At the forefront of those who foresaw the dangers which would accompany the integration of Eastern Europe, journalist Misha Glenny has added a new chapter to his well-known book, bringing it up-to-date.

Hašek, Jaroslav, *The Good Soldier Švejk and his Fortunes in the World War* (Penguin Modern Classics, London, 1983). Sir Cecil Parrott's translation is the first complete English edition recounting the exploits of a Mr Everyman pitted against Central European bureaucracy. Illustrated by Hašek's friend, Josef Lada.

(preceding pages) Demonstrations in the Old Town Square, December 1989

Havel, Václav, *Living in Truth*, edited by Jan Vladislav (Faber and Faber, London, 1989). Once persecuted and censored, Havel was elected President of the Czech Republic. This book, along with his *Letters to Olga*, celebrates Havel's fight for freedom of thought, publicly launched in his letter to Gustáv Husák, General Secretary of the Czechoslovak Communist Party and Charter '77.

Jirásek, Alois, *Old Czech Legends* (Forest Books, London, 1992). A collection of all the classic Czech legends which popularized Bohemia's past.

Kafka, Franz, *The Diaries of Franz Kafka 1910–22* edited by Max Brod (Penguin Modern Classics, London, 1972). The diaries, edited by a close friend, reveal the extraordinary inner world Kafka inhabited, interspersed with glimpses of real life.

Kundera, Milan, *The Book of Laughter and Forgetting*, translated by Philip Roth (Penguin, London, 1983). With his other novels such as *The Unbearable Lightness of Being* and *The Joke*, Milan Kundera brings us a searing insight into life as a Czech, a hedonist and a political satirist.

Rilke, Rainer Maria, *Selected Poems of Rainer Maria Rilke* translated by Robert Bly (Harper & Row, New York, 1981). This collection charts the development and explorations of Rilke as he breaks out of the claustrophobic atmosphere of his home to visit Moscow, Italy and Paris. Notable is the *Book of Pictures*, in which Rilke uses painting techniques in the composition of his poems.

Weil, Jiří, *Life with a Star* translated by Rita Klímová and Roslyn Schloss (Flamingo, London, 1990). A poignant memorial to the life of the Czech Jews under the Nazis, told with a stunning clarity by someone who experienced these terrible events first hand.

Child of Europe—A New Anthology of East European Poetry (Penguin, London). Contains translations of many poets hitherto inaccessible to non-Czech speakers.

Index

Looking south along the Tepla, Karlovy Vary